LITTLE BOOKS
ABOUT BIG THINGS

WORLD RELIGIONS

LITTLE BOOKS
ABOUT
BIG
THINGS

WORLD
RELIGIONS

VICTOR DORFF

FALL RIVER PRESS

New York

FALL RIVER PRESS

New York

An Imprint of Sterling Publishing
387 Park Avenue South
New York, NY 10016

Interior design by Danielle Deschenes

Photos: © Depositphotos, © Fotolia, © iStockphoto, Wikimedia

ISBN 978-1-4351-4679-2

Distributed in Canada by Sterling Publishing
c/o Canadian Manda Group, 165 Dufferin Street
Toronto, Ontario, Canada M6K 3H6
Distributed in the United Kingdom by GMC Distribution Services
Castle Place, 166 High Street, Lewes, East Sussex, England BN7 1XU
Distributed in Australia by Capricorn Link (Australia) Pty. Ltd.
P.O. Box 704, Windsor, NSW 2756, Australia

For information about custom editions, special sales, and premium and
corporate purchases, please contact Sterling Special Sales at 800-805-5489 or
specialsales@sterlingpublishing.com.

Manufactured in China

2 4 6 8 10 9 7 5 3 1

www.sterlingpublishing.com

DEDICATION

To all the Agnostics, Atheists, Buddhists, Catholics, Deists, Episcopalians, Jews, Lutherans, Methodists, Mormons, and Undecideds who make up my family, and to all of my friends, who round out the rest of the faiths.

For as long as humans have existed, religions have provided reasons to live, reasons to die, and reasons to kill.

For some, religion offers comfort and guidance from a power beyond themselves. Others see religion as a way to differentiate themselves from those who follow a different path.

Humans turn to religion to answer the most difficult questions: Why am I here? What should I do? Who shapes my destiny?

Every religion tells a story of mankind's quest for something—eternal life, infinite wisdom, profound peace, or perhaps an understanding of the true meaning of existence.

Some religions build on existing religions by extending the story or modifying some portion of it. Others create new stories that attract followers who hear a ring of truth in those stories.

Within the pages that follow, all religions—large and small, established and fringe, ongoing and defunct—are treated as equally holy, because for everything written here, there is someone, somewhere, who considers it gospel.

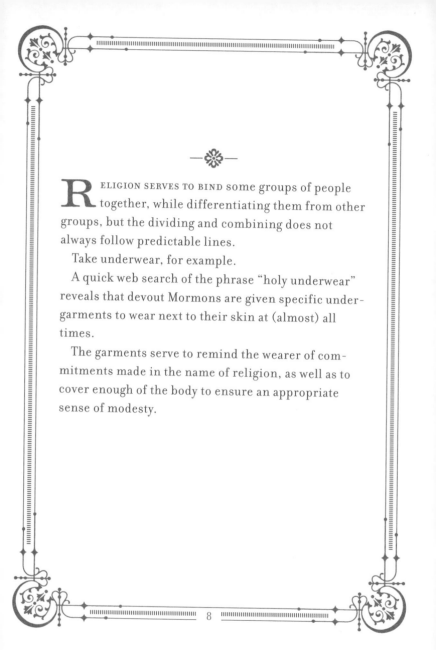

—✿—

R ELIGION SERVES TO BIND some groups of people together, while differentiating them from other groups, but the dividing and combining does not always follow predictable lines.

Take underwear, for example.

A quick web search of the phrase "holy underwear" reveals that devout Mormons are given specific undergarments to wear next to their skin at (almost) all times.

The garments serve to remind the wearer of commitments made in the name of religion, as well as to cover enough of the body to ensure an appropriate sense of modesty.

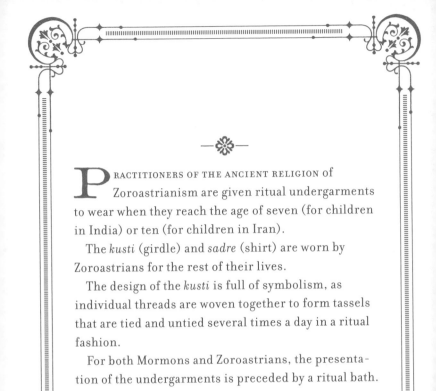

PRACTITIONERS OF THE ANCIENT RELIGION of Zoroastrianism are given ritual undergarments to wear when they reach the age of seven (for children in India) or ten (for children in Iran).

The *kusti* (girdle) and *sadre* (shirt) are worn by Zoroastrians for the rest of their lives.

The design of the *kusti* is full of symbolism, as individual threads are woven together to form tassels that are tied and untied several times a day in a ritual fashion.

For both Mormons and Zoroastrians, the presentation of the undergarments is preceded by a ritual bath.

ONE OF THE COMMANDMENTS GIVEN by God to the Hebrews is the mandate for men to wear tzitzit (tassels) with a blue cord on the corners of all their garments.

The tassels serve as a constant reminder of the connection between the Jews and their Lord.

These days, most garments don't have corners, so Orthodox Jews wear a *Tallit Katan* (a four-cornered undergarment) onto which they attach their tzitzit.

P RAYER BEADS ARE USED in many religions to help the faithful keep track of their prayers.

In Islam, the *misbaha* or *tasbih* have ninety-nine or thirty-three beads.

Hindus use a string of 108 or twenty-seven beads, and Buddhists and Sikhs appear to have continued that practice.

The Baha'i bead-count is nineteen or ninety-five, with an additional five beads tacked on.

Roman Catholics use a rosary that has fifty-four beads, plus an extra five.

T HE MOST RECENT ESTIMATES of the U.S. Central
Intelligence Agency say that one-third of the
world's population (33.39 percent of 7 billion people)
are Christians.

The CIA provides the following further breakdown
on sects of Christianity:

ROMAN CATHOLIC ⇐	16.85%
PROTESTANT ⇐	6.15%
ORTHODOX ⇐	3.96%
ANGLICAN ⇐	1.26%
OTHER ⇐	5.17%

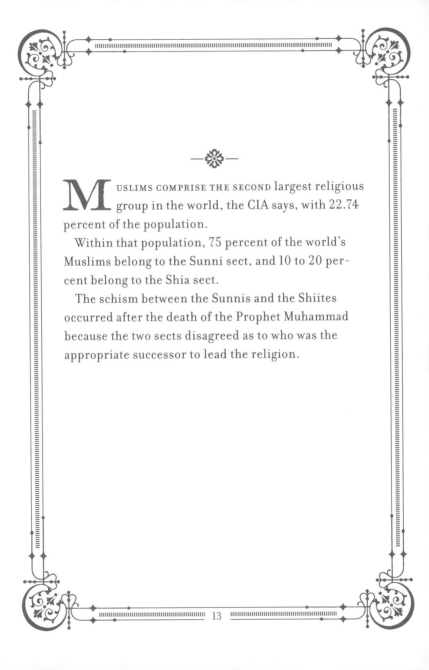

MUSLIMS COMPRISE THE SECOND largest religious group in the world, the CIA says, with 22.74 percent of the population.

Within that population, 75 percent of the world's Muslims belong to the Sunni sect, and 10 to 20 percent belong to the Shia sect.

The schism between the Sunnis and the Shiites occurred after the death of the Prophet Muhammad because the two sects disagreed as to who was the appropriate successor to lead the religion.

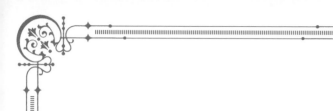

T HE REMAINING PEOPLE of the world divide themselves as:

HINDU ⇐ 13.8%
BUDDHIST ⇐ 6.7%
SIKH ⇐ 0.35%
JEWISH ⇐ 0.22%
BAHA'I ⇐ 0.11%
OTHER ⇐ 10.95%
NONRELIGIOUS ⇐ 9.66%
ATHEISTS ⇐ 2.01%

Which religion holds that the gods tried and failed repeatedly to create the world, finally succeeding on the fifth try (at the cost of their own lives)?

The Aztecs believed that infighting among the gods prevented the first four attempts at creating the world from succeeding.

Each time a god began creating, another god knocked the sun out of the sky and destroyed the world.

On the fifth try, they worked together and succeeded.

IN THE FINAL ATTEMPT to make the world, *two* Aztec gods sacrificed themselves to become suns.

Two suns made it too hot for the world to survive, so the remaining gods threw a rabbit in the face of the second sun god.

That dimmed the second sun, which became the moon—destined to follow the sun and never be as bright.

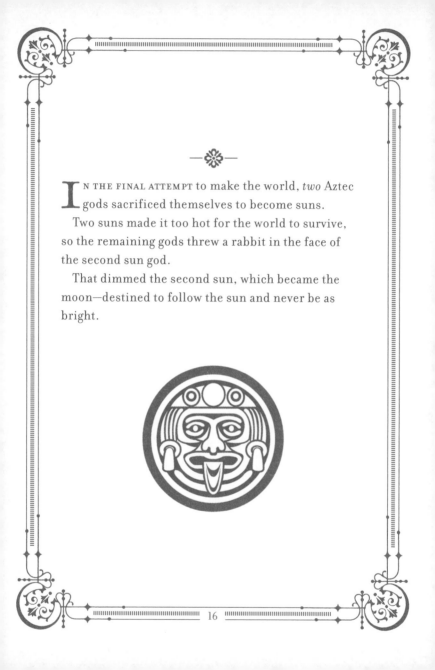

—❧—

ALTHOUGH IT IS BELIEVED THAT MANY of the Aztec sacrifice victims went voluntarily for the opportunity to serve their gods, the act of sacrificing them was exceptionally violent.

The beating hearts of the sacrifices were removed and held up to the gods, and the bodies were thrown down the stairs of the temple.

Some even say the bodies were dragged off by the local residents and eaten.

POP QUIZ

How many human sacrifices did the Aztecs make to their gods each year?

a. One virgin sacrifice at the beginning of each year
b. One sacrifice of an enemy warrior for each equinox and solstice
c. Tens of thousands, including prisoners, conquered warriors, and volunteer Aztecs
d. Each community sacrificed one volunteer at every new moon

ANSWER: c.

According to estimates in contemporary records, Aztec gods had a voracious appetite for human blood.

T HE APPETITE OF THE AZTECS (or their gods) for human blood was so great, there were not enough volunteers.

To keep the gods sated, the Aztecs made a deal with a neighboring city-state to enter combat for the purpose of taking prisoners for sacrifice.

Both the Aztecs and the Tlaxcalans worshipped the same gods, and their ritual battles, called the Flowery Wars, were about feeding those gods, not about land or conquest.

The practice ended when the Spanish came; the Tlaxcala people joined the Spanish in defeating the Aztecs.

In America, who are more likely to be atheists,
men or women?

Of those who identify themselves as atheists, 70 percent are men. Men also make up 75 percent of the agnostics and 58 percent of those who say they have no religion.

Even international studies show that men tend to be more secular than women.

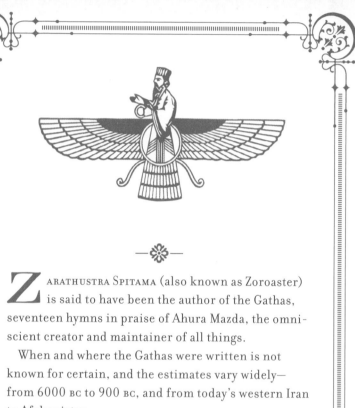

ZARATHUSTRA SPITAMA (also known as Zoroaster) is said to have been the author of the Gathas, seventeen hymns in praise of Ahura Mazda, the omniscient creator and maintainer of all things.

When and where the Gathas were written is not known for certain, and the estimates vary widely—from 6000 BC to 900 BC, and from today's western Iran to Afghanistan.

The Gathas form the central text of Zoroastrianism, believed by its followers to be the first monotheistic religion.

T HE ZOROASTRIANS BELIEVE THAT MANY of their religious tenets—the duality of good and evil, the coming of a savior born of a virgin, the promise of resurrection and judgment at the End of Days— have found their way into modern-day Judaism, Christianity, and Islam.

Some maintain that the Magi mentioned in the Christian gospels were actually Zoroastrians who had traveled from Persia.

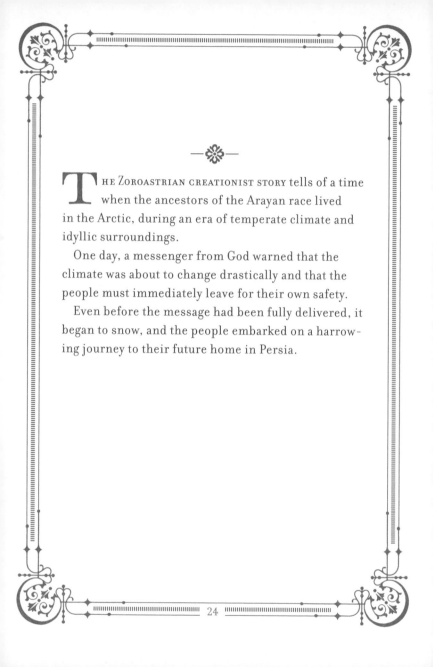

THE ZOROASTRIAN CREATIONIST STORY tells of a time when the ancestors of the Arayan race lived in the Arctic, during an era of temperate climate and idyllic surroundings.

One day, a messenger from God warned that the climate was about to change drastically and that the people must immediately leave for their own safety.

Even before the message had been fully delivered, it began to snow, and the people embarked on a harrowing journey to their future home in Persia.

WHEN THE MUSLIMS CONQUERED PERSIA, the Zoroastrians were persecuted until they converted or left.

Today, few Zoroastrians are left in Iran. Most are found in India, where they are known as Parsis.

In fact, there are few Zoroastrians left worldwide, in part because they traditionally discourage conversion and marriage outside the religion.

Conversion is thought to be an affront to God, because all religions are equally good and a person's birth-religion is seen as a gift from God.

IN 1774, THE FIRST MEMBERS of an English Quaker splinter group (United Society of Believers in Christ's Second Appearing) settled in upstate New York.

Known as Shakers, members of this sect believe in a form of religious communism: all property is jointly owned, and the community shares in the fruits of its labors.

As pacifists, the Shakers did not approve of the Colonists' revolt against the British.

During the Civil War, Abraham Lincoln exempted members of the Shaker sect from the military draft, making them the first of the nation's "conscientious objectors."

Although the sympathy of the Shakers tended to lie with the Union, both Confederate and Union soldiers were welcomed and cared for in Shaker communities.

LINCOLN

SHAKERS EMBRACE CELIBACY and reject procreation, so the growth of the movement came only through conversion and adoption.

Today, the Shakers are nearly extinct.

As of Spring 2013, there are three living Shakers.

They reside in the only remaining community, which is in Sabbathday Lake, Maine.

I N THEIR STATEMENT OF BASIC PRINCIPLES and beliefs, the remaining Shakers say,

"Shakerism is not, as many would claim, an anachronism; nor can it be dismissed as the final sad flowering of nineteenth-century liberal utopian fervor...

   "It teaches above all else that God is Love and that our most solemn duty is to show forth that God, who is Love in the World...

   "It values human fulfillment highly and believes that we fulfill ourselves best by being nothing more nor less than ourselves... [W]e cannot be disillusioned with people being themselves."

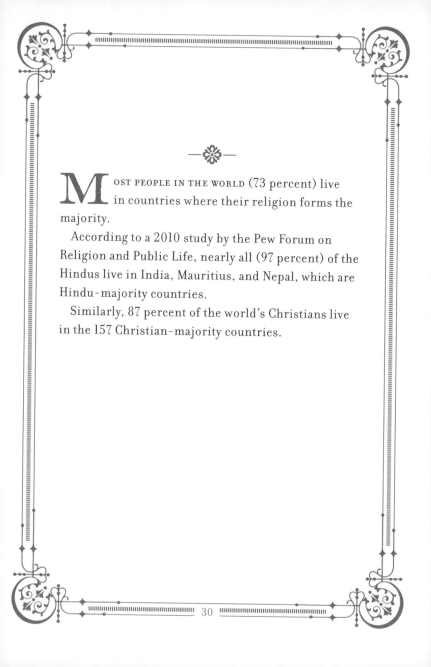

MOST PEOPLE IN THE WORLD (73 percent) live in countries where their religion forms the majority.

According to a 2010 study by the Pew Forum on Religion and Public Life, nearly all (97 percent) of the Hindus live in India, Mauritius, and Nepal, which are Hindu-majority countries.

Similarly, 87 percent of the world's Christians live in the 157 Christian-majority countries.

J UST AS THE RELIGIOUS TEND to live with like-minded people, the religiously unaffiliated also tend to live in countries where they make up the majority—China, Czech Republic, Estonia, Hong Kong, Japan, and North Korea.

There are twice as many "religiously unaffiliated" people in China (700 million) as there are people of *any* religion living in the United States.

The Pew Forum on Religion & Public Life says that more than 400 million people (about 6 percent of the world's population) practice folk/traditional religions—African, Chinese, Native American, and Australian aboriginal.

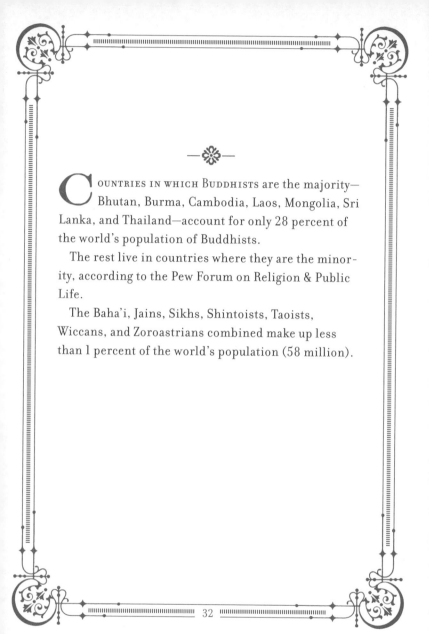

COUNTRIES IN WHICH BUDDHISTS are the majority—Bhutan, Burma, Cambodia, Laos, Mongolia, Sri Lanka, and Thailand—account for only 28 percent of the world's population of Buddhists.

The rest live in countries where they are the minority, according to the Pew Forum on Religion & Public Life.

The Baha'i, Jains, Sikhs, Shintoists, Taoists, Wiccans, and Zoroastrians combined make up less than 1 percent of the world's population (58 million).

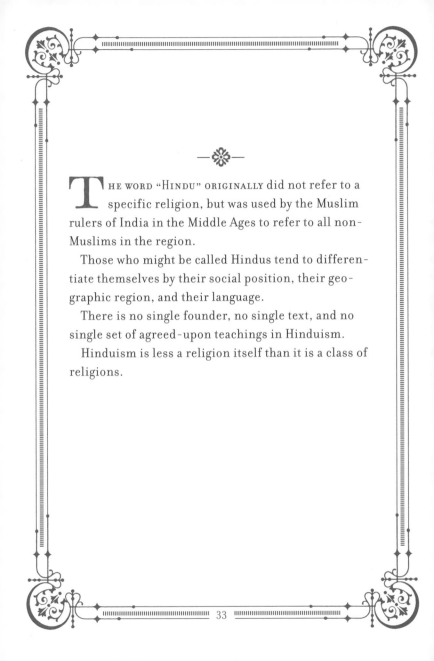

The word "Hindu" originally did not refer to a specific religion, but was used by the Muslim rulers of India in the Middle Ages to refer to all non-Muslims in the region.

Those who might be called Hindus tend to differentiate themselves by their social position, their geographic region, and their language.

There is no single founder, no single text, and no single set of agreed-upon teachings in Hinduism.

Hinduism is less a religion itself than it is a class of religions.

T HE OLDEST HINDU TEACHINGS, the Vedas ("knowledge"), are thousands of years old.

They are believed to have been received directly
from God and passed on orally from generation to
generation.

The Vedas in their present form date back to around
1200 BC and contain hymns, poems, and instructions
on how to conduct ritual sacrifices.

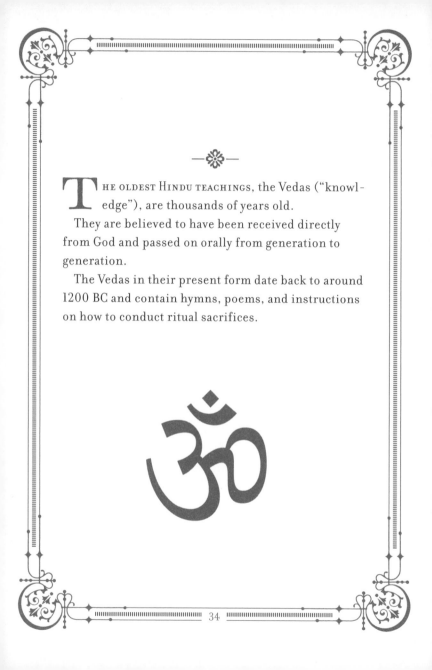

THE UPANISHADS ("SITTING NEAR THE TEACHER") are more than one hundred additional texts that were added to the Vedas around 700–800 BC.

The Upanishads include poetry, scientific discussions, and dialogues on metaphysical issues.

These combined texts introduce the concepts of the soul (atman) and a Supreme Being (Brahman) and the relationship between the two.

ONE OF THE UPANISHADS CONSISTS of a dialogue in which a father instructs his son to dissolve some salt into a bowl of water. Although the salt disappears and cannot be retrieved, one taste reveals that it is still present in the water.

The father likens the salt to the atman (immortal soul) and the water to Brahman (Supreme Being), explaining that the essence of the Self exists within the undivided whole of the Supreme Being.

Pointing to the salt water, the father says, "You are that."

T HE BHAGAVAD GITA ("SONG OF THE BLESSED ONE") is considered one of the holiest books of Hinduism.

It is a dialogue between Krishna, who is a human manifestation of the Supreme Being, and a soldier about to engage in battle against an army of friends and family.

The soldier puts down his weapons and refuses to fight.

Krishna explains the moral imperative of fighting for what is right and how selfless action can lead to "liberation," or release from the cycle of birth, death, and reincarnation.

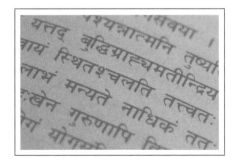

According to FBI statistics for the year 2011, 6,216 "single-bias" hate crime incidents were recorded.

Religious bias was behind 19.8 percent of the cases—the third-most frequent motivation.

Racial bias came in first, accounting for nearly half of the incidents (46.9 percent).

Sexual orientation bias was second, at 20.8 percent.

Ethnicity and national origin bias came fourth, at 11.6 percent.

Disability bias was the least frequently cited cause, at 0.9 percent.

T HE SCRIPTURES OF BOTH JUDAISM and Islam have a
number of specific references about how wars
should be fought.

In the Torah, God admonishes not to be afraid of the
enemy in wartime, because He will ensure victory.

In the Quran, Allah warns believers not to run from
nonbelievers in battle, for they will incur His wrath.

Both scriptures also recommend, as a general rule,
to accept peace with an enemy who is truly willing to
come to terms.

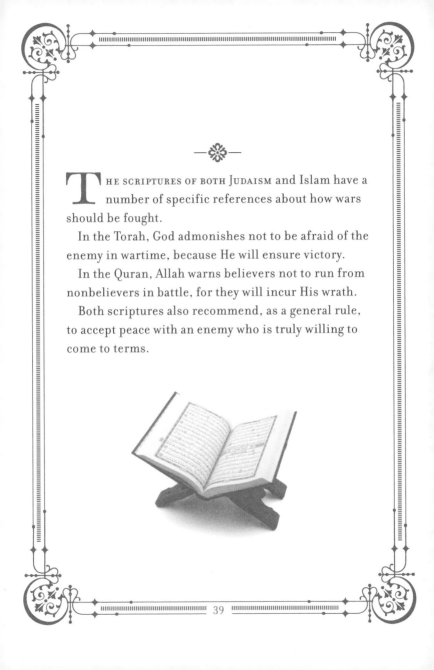

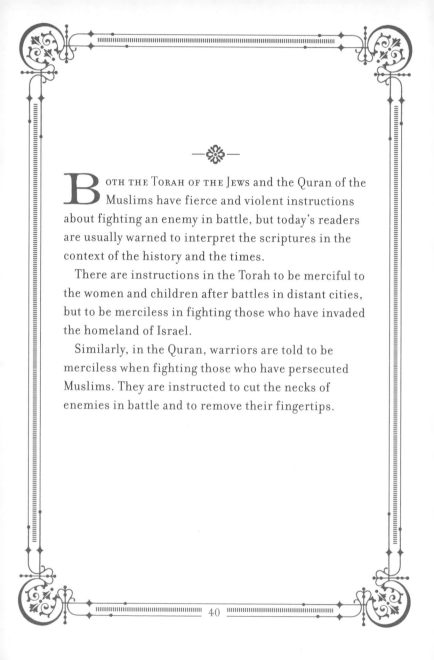

Bᴏᴛʜ ᴛʜᴇ Tᴏʀᴀʜ ᴏғ ᴛʜᴇ Jᴇᴡs and the Quran of the Muslims have fierce and violent instructions about fighting an enemy in battle, but today's readers are usually warned to interpret the scriptures in the context of the history and the times.

There are instructions in the Torah to be merciful to the women and children after battles in distant cities, but to be merciless in fighting those who have invaded the homeland of Israel.

Similarly, in the Quran, warriors are told to be merciless when fighting those who have persecuted Muslims. They are instructed to cut the necks of enemies in battle and to remove their fingertips.

G LOBALLY, JEWS ARE THE RELIGIOUS GROUP with the highest median age (thirty-six years old), and Muslims are the youngest (twenty-three years old).

The Pew Forum on Religion & Public Life says that, on average, the world's Hindus are twenty-six years old, the Christians are thirty years old, and the Buddhists are thirty-four years old.

Within the scriptures two religions have specific instructions not to harm fruit-bearing trees in time of war. Which are they? The third tells of a time when a hungry holy man approached a fruit tree not in season, found there was no food to be had, and killed the tree. Which is it?

a. Christianity
b. Islam
c. Judaism
d. Hinduism

A N S W E R S : b. Islam (Jihad 21.3.10) and c. Judaism (Deut. 20:19-20) enjoin destruction of fruit trees.

a. Christianity. On finding that a fig tree had no fruit to eat, Jesus cursed it, and it was withered and dead the next day. (Mark 11:12-25)

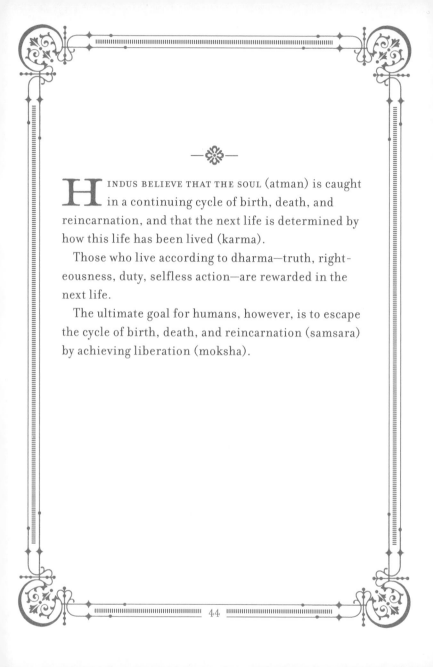

HINDUS BELIEVE THAT THE SOUL (atman) is caught in a continuing cycle of birth, death, and reincarnation, and that the next life is determined by how this life has been lived (karma).

Those who live according to dharma—truth, righteousness, duty, selfless action—are rewarded in the next life.

The ultimate goal for humans, however, is to escape the cycle of birth, death, and reincarnation (samsara) by achieving liberation (moksha).

IN THE BHAGAVAD GITA, Krishna explains that there are three paths to reach God and achieve liberation: devotion, knowledge, or selfless action.

Each of these paths (or a combination of all three) may lead to the extermination of one's karma, which allows the atman (individual soul) to return to its state of unity with the Brahman.

Many Hindus attempt to lead lives of complete devotion to one of many deities (any one of which represents a manifestation of the Brahman) as the way to escape samsara (the cycle of birth, death, and reincarnation).

Is Hare Krishna a real religion?

Yes. In 1965, at the age of 69, Abhay Charan De arrived in New York City as a Hindu immigrant from India.

On his arrival he began to spread the message of his religion to the English-speaking world.

Less than a year later, he founded the International Society for Krishna Consciousness and launched the Hare Krishna movement.

The Society now has more than 100 temples, ashrams, and cultural centers worldwide.

—❧—

D ANCE AND MUSIC ARE HIGHLY VALUED in the
Hindu world as expressions of divinity.

Dedicated performers are thought to be pursuing
another path to liberation, as music is believed to be a
manifestation of Brahman (the Supreme Being) in the
form of sound.

Much of Hindu worship includes re-creating sacred
stories in song and dance. In fact, the performers
themselves are considered divine during such perfor-
mances.

I N THE SIXTH CENTURY BC, as the Upanishads were being written, some scholars were questioning the elitist nature of Hinduism.

The holy texts were all written in Sanskrit, the language of the upper castes, and were inaccessible to much of the population.

Enter Siddhartha Gautama and Mahavira, who both rejected the orthodoxy of Hinduism and taught in the languages of the people.

Siddhartha became Buddha.

Mahavira developed Jainism.

JAINISM CALLS UPON ITS FOLLOWERS to achieve their own liberation from samsara. There are no deities to help in the process.

Souls that have achieved moksha (liberation) are not thought of as gods, but as teachers whose souls developed into the ultimate, pure state.

Twenty-four of those who reached liberation are called Tirthankaras, because they provided a modified path to enlightenment.

Mahavira (Great Hero) was the last of the Tirthankaras.

J AINS DO *not* BELIEVE IN A GOD who created the universe, maintains the universe, or sits in judgment of human souls.

A perfect being would feel no need to create a universe and would not require worship from people.

In fact, all souls have the potential to become perfect—at which point, they would no longer have any interest in worldly affairs and would be beyond the reach of human prayer.

J AINS BELIEVE THAT ALL ANIMALS and plants have souls that are no less valuable than the human soul.

For this reason, Jains are usually not just vegetarians, but they also restrict their diets to fruits and nuts.

Even microbes have souls, so many Jains wear masks to avoid breathing them in and harming them.

In addition to nonviolence, Jains believe in limiting their impact on the world by restricting their travel and use of resources, so as to minimize any damage they do to living creatures.

Followers of Jainism take the following vows:

→ *Ahimsa*: nonviolence in thought, word, and deed
→ *Satya*: truthfulness and honesty
→ *Achaurya*: no cheating, stealing, or avoiding of taxes
→ *Bramacharya*: chastity, except within marriage, and then only for the purpose of giving birth to a son
→ *Aparigraha*: to live simply, possessing only what is necessary

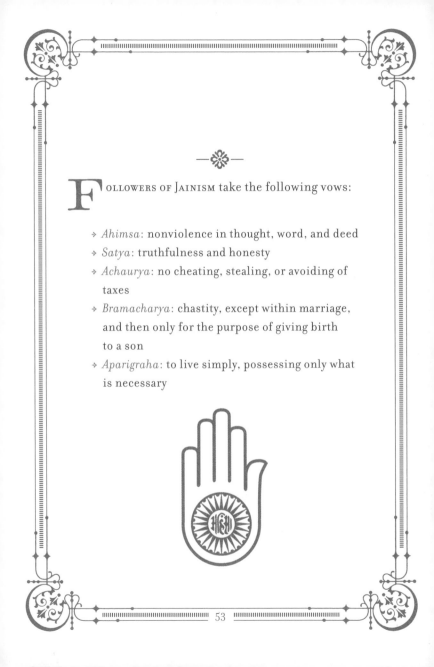

J AINS DO NOT PRAY TO ASK FOR ANYTHING, but to show reverence to those who have attained—or who are on the path toward—enlightenment.

The most important prayer in Jainism is the Namokar Mantra:

> ⇢ I bow before the enlightened ones.
> ⇢ I bow before the perfected ones.
> ⇢ I bow before the spiritual leaders.
> ⇢ I bow before the spiritual teachers.
> ⇢ I bow before all spiritual practitioners.
> ⇢ This fivefold repetition destroys all bad karmas
>   and is the most auspicious of all mantras.

MOST AMERICAN ADULTS BELIEVE IN GOD (82 percent), in miracles (76 percent), in heaven (75 percent), that Jesus is God or the son of God (73 percent), in angels (72 percent), that the soul survives after death (71 percent), in the resurrection of Jesus (70 percent), in hell (61 percent), and in the devil (60 percent).

Less than half (45 percent) believe in Darwin's theory of evolution.

The same Harris Poll found:

> * 42% believe in ghosts
> * 32% believe in UFOs
> * 26% believe in astrology
> * 23% believe in witches
> * 20% believe they were someone
>   else in another life

POP QUIZ

According to the American Religious Identification Survey, which religion saw the biggest percentage increase in population from 1990 to 2008?

a. Buddhism
b. Christianity
c. Judaism
d. Islam

ANSWER: a. Buddhism

B UDDHISM IS THE OUTCOME of the spiritual quest of Siddhartha Gautama.

In the sixth century BC, he was born a prince in the area that is Nepal today, and he was raised in a life of privilege and luxury.

On his first venture outside the walls of his royal compound, he encountered "suffering": the aged, the sick, and the dead.

The experience prompted him to embark on a quest to find the cause of suffering and a way to end it.

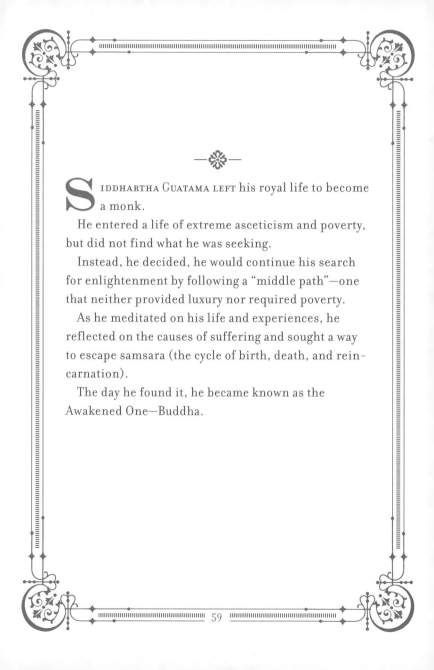

SIDDHARTHA GUATAMA LEFT his royal life to become a monk.

He entered a life of extreme asceticism and poverty, but did not find what he was seeking.

Instead, he decided, he would continue his search for enlightenment by following a "middle path"—one that neither provided luxury nor required poverty.

As he meditated on his life and experiences, he reflected on the causes of suffering and sought a way to escape samsara (the cycle of birth, death, and reincarnation).

The day he found it, he became known as the Awakened One—Buddha.

T HE GOD OF ABRAHAM COMMANDED his followers to
obey a core list of rules.

Jews believe that God issued not ten, but 613 commandments to Moses, and that each of those commandments falls into categories delineated by what
are generally referred to as "the Ten Commandments."

Initially, the Ten Commandments were written by
the finger of God into two tablets of stone and given to
Moses, who dropped and broke them.

THE TEN COMMANDMENTS
(Judaism)

1. I am the Lord, thy God, who brought thee out of slavery in the land of Egypt.
2. Thou shalt have no other gods before me nor make for thyself graven images.
3. Thou shalt not take the name of the Lord, thy God, in vain.
4. Remember the Sabbath and keep it holy.
5. Honor thy father and mother.
6. Thou shalt not murder.
7. Thou shalt not commit adultery.
8. Thou shalt not steal.
9. Thou shalt not bear false witness against thy neighbor.
10. Thou shalt not covet thy neighbor's wife nor anything belonging to thy neighbor.

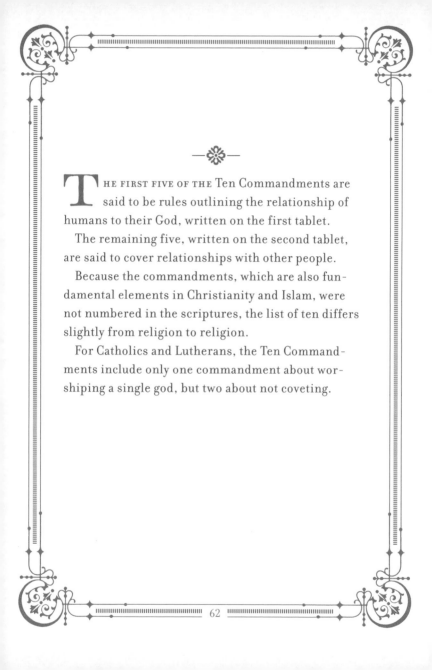

—❧—

T HE FIRST FIVE OF THE Ten Commandments are said to be rules outlining the relationship of humans to their God, written on the first tablet.

The remaining five, written on the second tablet, are said to cover relationships with other people.

Because the commandments, which are also fundamental elements in Christianity and Islam, were not numbered in the scriptures, the list of ten differs slightly from religion to religion.

For Catholics and Lutherans, the Ten Commandments include only one commandment about worshiping a single god, but two about not coveting.

THE TEN COMMANDMENTS
(St. Augustine)

1. I am the Lord, your God. You shall have no strange gods before me.
2. You shall not take the name of the Lord, your God, in vain.
3. Remember to keep holy the Lord's Day.
4. Honor your father and your mother.
5. You shall not kill.
6. You shall not commit adultery.
7. You shall not steal.
8. You shall not bear false witness against your neighbor.
9. You shall not covet your neighbor's wife.
10. You shall not covet your neighbor's goods.

SUBSEQUENT PROTESTANT RELIGIONS viewed the phrase, "I am the Lord, thy God," as more of a prologue to the commandments than as a commandment itself, so it was removed from the first commandment.

Their restatement of the Ten Commandments re-emphasized the prohibition of idolatry by making it a separate commandment, in a direct rebuke to the Catholic tradition of saints, statues, and religious artifacts.

To keep the number of commandments at the traditional ten, however, the Protestants recombined the two prohibitions against coveting.

THE TEN COMMANDMENTS
(King James Bible)

1. Thou shalt have no other gods before me.
2. Thou shalt not make unto thee any graven image.
3. Thou shalt not take the name of the Lord thy God in vain.
4. Remember the Sabbath day, to keep it holy.
5. Honor thy father and thy mother.
6. Thou shalt not kill.
7. Thou shalt not commit adultery.
8. Thou shalt not steal.
9. Thou shalt not bear false witness against thy neighbor.
10. Thou shalt not covet…anything that is thy neighbor's.

ALTHOUGH THE CHRISTIAN RELIGIONS adopted the Ten Commandments, Jews believe that only *they* are actually bound by all ten.

In Judaism, a separate (and less strict) set of *seven* commandments applies to the human race in general.

Six of those commandments are inferred from the story of Adam in the Garden of Eden. The seventh was added when God instructed Noah and his family to repopulate the earth after a massive flood had killed everyone else.

THE NOAHIDE LAWS

(The Seven Laws for Mankind)

1. Don't worship idols.
2. Don't murder.
3. Don't steal.
4. Don't commit immoral sexual acts.
5. Don't commit blasphemy.
6. Create courts and a system of legal recourse.
7. Don't eat flesh taken from an animal while it is still alive.

THE MORAL AND ETHICAL CODE of Buddhism is contained in the Five Precepts, which all followers are expected to adopt:

1. No killing.
2. No stealing.
3. No sexual misconduct.
4. No improper speech.
5. No intoxicating substances.

BUDDHA TAUGHT THAT NOTHING is permanent and that change is inevitable.

Suffering (or dissatisfaction), he said, is a result of our quest for something—happiness, fulfillment, etc.—that will last, but nothing does.

He identified Four Noble Truths that summarize his findings:

1. Life is suffering or dissatisfaction.
2. Suffering/dissatisfaction is caused by desires/ craving/thirst.
3. Suffering/dissatisfaction can be ended.
4. There is a path that leads to the end of suffering/ dissatisfaction.

The Four Noble Truths are sometimes cast in the form of a physician attending to a patient:

By identifying life's suffering, Buddha makes a diagnosis.

By identifying the cause of suffering, Buddha isolates the cause of the illness.

By saying that suffering can be eliminated, Buddha promises a return to full health.

In identifying a method of eliminating suffering, Buddha is issuing a prescription to be followed.

That prescription is enumerated in the Noble Eightfold Path.

THE NOBLE EIGHTFOLD PATH

+ RIGHT VIEW: an understanding of the Four Noble Truths
+ RIGHT INTENTIONS: to renounce attachments and aversions; to embrace compassion
+ RIGHT SPEECH: to eschew lies, insults, anger, gossip
+ RIGHT ACTION: not to steal, to kill, or to engage in sexual misconduct
+ RIGHT LIVELIHOOD: to earn one's living without hurting others
+ RIGHT EFFORT: to work toward maintaining a wholesome mind
+ RIGHT MINDFULNESS: awareness of one's thoughts, feelings, and reactions
+ RIGHT CONCENTRATION: focus on the goal of eliminating suffering/dissatisfaction

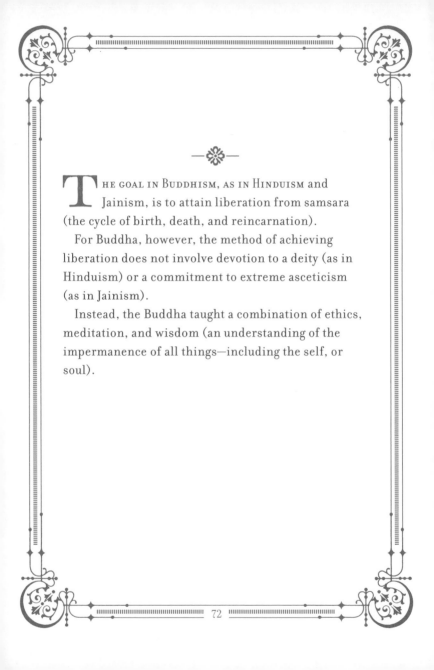

—❊—

THE GOAL IN BUDDHISM, AS IN HINDUISM and Jainism, is to attain liberation from samsara (the cycle of birth, death, and reincarnation).

For Buddha, however, the method of achieving liberation does not involve devotion to a deity (as in Hinduism) or a commitment to extreme asceticism (as in Jainism).

Instead, the Buddha taught a combination of ethics, meditation, and wisdom (an understanding of the impermanence of all things—including the self, or soul).

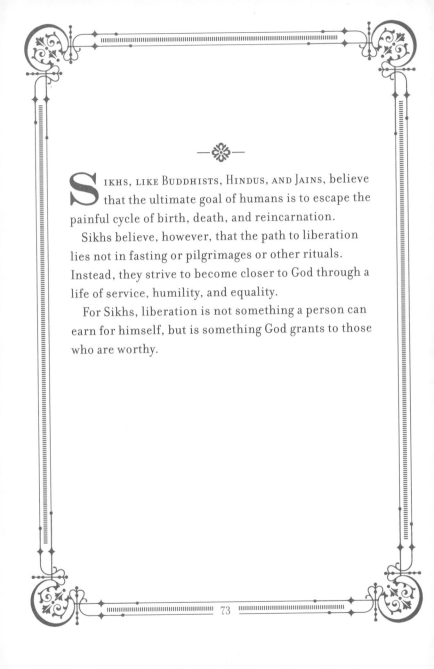

—❀—

S IKHS, LIKE BUDDHISTS, HINDUS, AND JAINS, believe
that the ultimate goal of humans is to escape the
painful cycle of birth, death, and reincarnation.

Sikhs believe, however, that the path to liberation
lies not in fasting or pilgrimages or other rituals.
Instead, they strive to become closer to God through a
life of service, humility, and equality.

For Sikhs, liberation is not something a person can
earn for himself, but is something God grants to those
who are worthy.

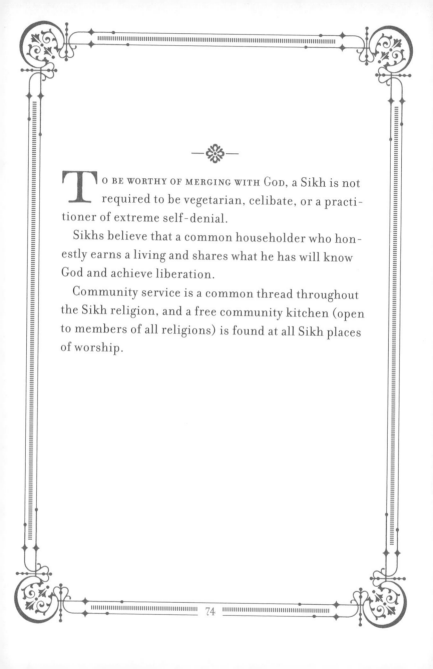

T O BE WORTHY OF MERGING WITH GOD, a Sikh is not required to be vegetarian, celibate, or a practitioner of extreme self-denial.

Sikhs believe that a common householder who honestly earns a living and shares what he has will know God and achieve liberation.

Community service is a common thread throughout the Sikh religion, and a free community kitchen (open to members of all religions) is found at all Sikh places of worship.

THE SIKH RELIGION WAS FOUNDED by Guru Nanak in the fifteenth century in the Punjab region of what is now India and Pakistan.

He was critical of the Hindu and Muslim rituals, and he preached a life of prayer, work, and giving.

Upon his death, Guru Nanak was followed by nine successive Gurus.

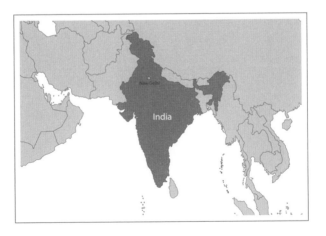

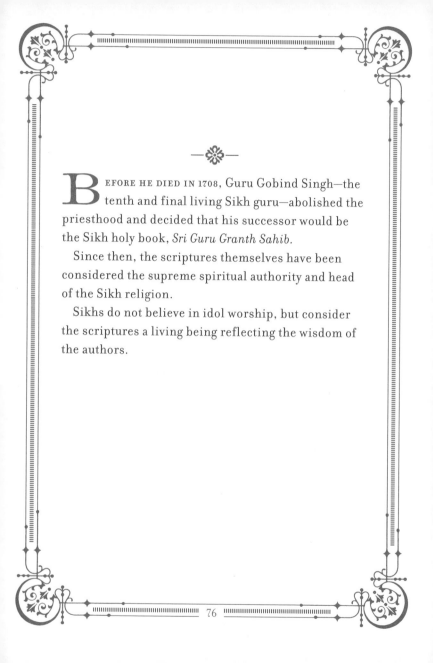

Before he died in 1708, Guru Gobind Singh—the tenth and final living Sikh guru—abolished the priesthood and decided that his successor would be the Sikh holy book, *Sri Guru Granth Sahib*.

Since then, the scriptures themselves have been considered the supreme spiritual authority and head of the Sikh religion.

Sikhs do not believe in idol worship, but consider the scriptures a living being reflecting the wisdom of the authors.

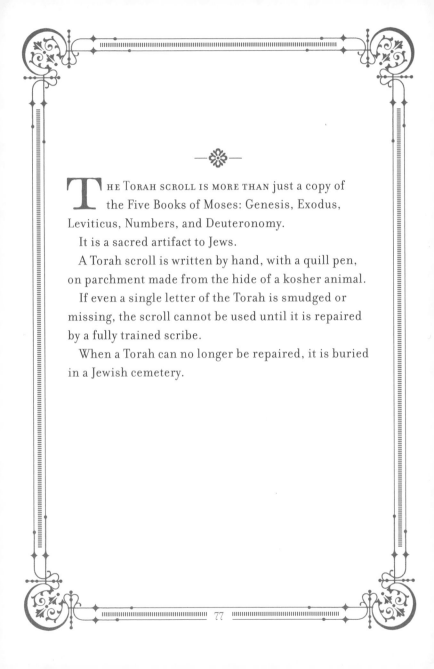

THE TORAH SCROLL IS MORE THAN just a copy of the Five Books of Moses: Genesis, Exodus, Leviticus, Numbers, and Deuteronomy.

It is a sacred artifact to Jews.

A Torah scroll is written by hand, with a quill pen, on parchment made from the hide of a kosher animal.

If even a single letter of the Torah is smudged or missing, the scroll cannot be used until it is repaired by a fully trained scribe.

When a Torah can no longer be repaired, it is buried in a Jewish cemetery.

During Jewish sabbath services, members of a synagogue are called to read a portion of the Torah.

The Torah is divided into portions in such a way that the entire text is read over the course of one year.

On any given day, in any temple anywhere in the world, the same portion of the Torah is being read.

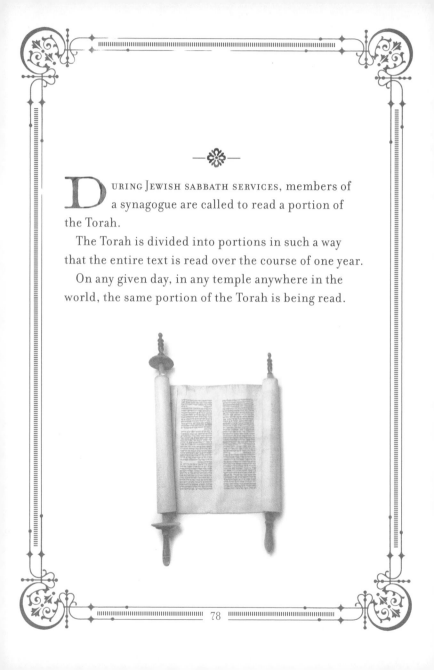

Do Jews believe in an afterlife?

Not much is specifically said about the afterlife in Judaism, other than that there is a World to Come (*Olam Ha-Ba*).

Beliefs vary and may include a notion of heaven and hell, while some maintain that the righteous will be rewarded and the wicked will simply be extinguished.

With 613 specific commandments and an extensive body of tradition developed around them, Judaism is primarily focused on living *this* life in accordance with the rules set forth in the covenant with God.

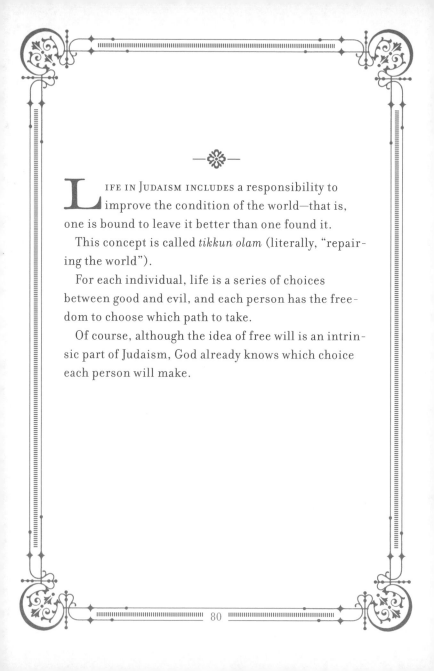

LIFE IN JUDAISM INCLUDES a responsibility to improve the condition of the world—that is, one is bound to leave it better than one found it.

This concept is called *tikkun olam* (literally, "repairing the world").

For each individual, life is a series of choices between good and evil, and each person has the freedom to choose which path to take.

Of course, although the idea of free will is an intrinsic part of Judaism, God already knows which choice each person will make.

THE CIA PROVIDES THE FOLLOWING statistics about the religious makeup of the U.S. population:

PROTESTANT ←	51.3%
ROMAN CATHOLIC ←	23.9%
MORMON ←	1.7%
OTHER CHRISTIAN ←	1.6%
JEWISH ←	1.7%
BUDDHIST ←	0.7%
MUSLIM ←	0.6%
OTHER/UNSPECIFIED ←	2.5%
UNAFFILIATED ←	12%
NONE ←	4%

POP QUIZ

According to the American Religious Identification Survey, which religion saw a decrease in population from 1990 to 2008?

a. Buddhism
b. Christianity
c. Judaism
d. Islam

ANSWER: c. Judaism

What is the Chinese word for "religion"?

Until the invasion of western culture in the late nineteenth century, the Chinese didn't have *any* word for
religion.

Taoism, Buddhism, and Confucianism were referred
to as the Three Teachings, and were not seen as mutually
exclusive.

With the introduction of Christianity, the linguistic
need arose, and *zongjiao* (literally, "ancestral teachings")
became the word for religion.

MT. SONGSHANG, near Dengfeng in Henan province, is the central sacred mountain of China.

The area was once thought to be the center of heaven and earth, and it is the site of remains of the oldest religious buildings in China.

The region was central in the development of Buddhism and Taoism in China, and the site is now on UNESCO's World Heritage List.

POP QUIZ

What do Chinese families feed Zao Jun, the Kitchen God, before burning him in effigy at the end of the year?

a. Ice cream, to cool the burning fire
b. Seeds, to provide prosperity for the coming year
c. Sweets, to encourage him to make a good report of their homes when he gets to heaven
d. Salt, out of gratitude for providing tasty food during the past year

ANSWER: c.

If the Kitchen God has nothing nice to say, sticky sweets may also serve to glue his mouth shut.

B EGUN IN CHINA, ABOUT 2,500 YEARS AGO, Taoism
posits that all things are connected through
a flow of energy called the Tao (roughly translated as
"the Way").

Some compare the relation of the Tao of the physical
universe to the water in a river—it has its own motion,
its own force, and its own direction.

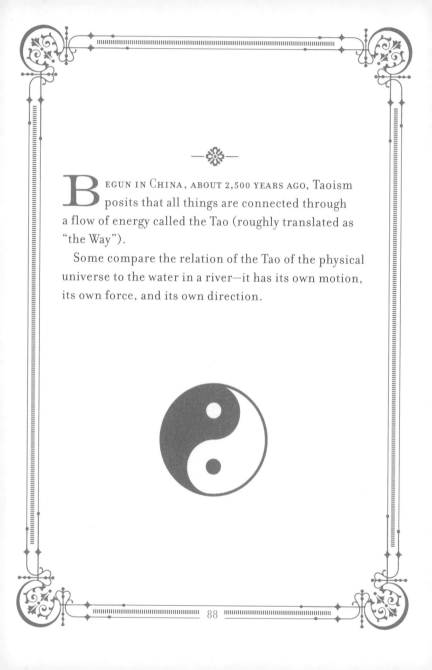

THE ESSENCE OF TAOISM is to come to understand that unifying force and to work *with* it, rather than *against* it—to allow events to unfold naturally, without trying to control them.

Taoism rejects emotionalism, rationalism, and physical sensations as methods for understanding and interpreting the world.

Instead, Taoism calls for attention to be paid to an inner world of spirituality, which it holds is a far superior vehicle for sensing the natural order of things.

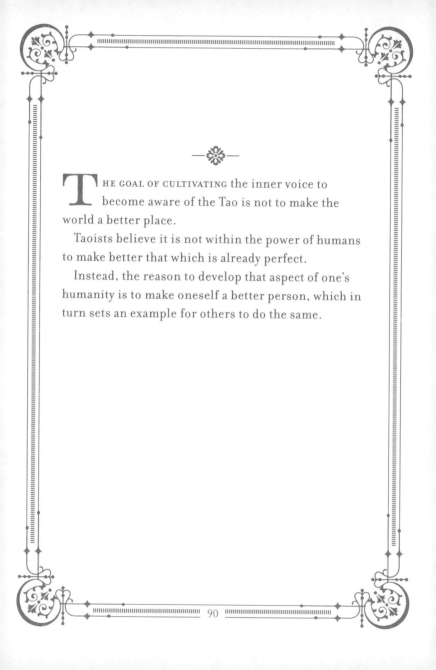

T HE GOAL OF CULTIVATING the inner voice to become aware of the Tao is not to make the world a better place.

Taoists believe it is not within the power of humans to make better that which is already perfect.

Instead, the reason to develop that aspect of one's humanity is to make oneself a better person, which in turn sets an example for others to do the same.

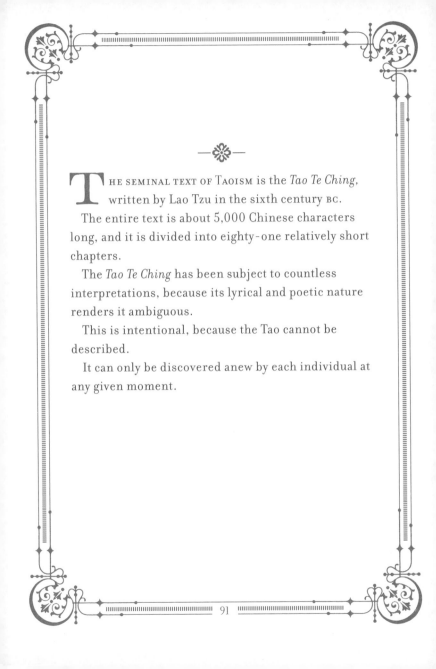

T HE SEMINAL TEXT OF TAOISM is the *Tao Te Ching*, written by Lao Tzu in the sixth century BC.

The entire text is about 5,000 Chinese characters long, and it is divided into eighty-one relatively short chapters.

The *Tao Te Ching* has been subject to countless interpretations, because its lyrical and poetic nature renders it ambiguous.

This is intentional, because the Tao cannot be described.

It can only be discovered anew by each individual at any given moment.

What is the Gourd of Chaos?

The Taoist story of Hundun (the "cosmic gourd") tells of the destruction of Chaos, seen as the perfected state, awash in endless possibilities.

Hundun was very generous to the Kings of the North and South, who felt compelled to repay him or lose face.

The Kings, obsessed about their debt, decided to repay the formless Hundun by puncturing him to give him eyes, nostrils, ears, and a mouth.

The result was the death of Hundun, which Taoists see as a case of slavish devotion to rules interfering with the Tao.

G"NOSIS" COMES FROM THE Greek word for "knowing," but knowing that doesn't really help explain Gnosticism.

There is disagreement as to whether Gnosticism is a form of Christianity or whether it predates Jesus.

There is disagreement as to whether it is pantheistic or monotheistic.

But what seems to be consistent in Gnostics is the belief that the creation of the world was a mistake (at best) or an act of evil (at worst).

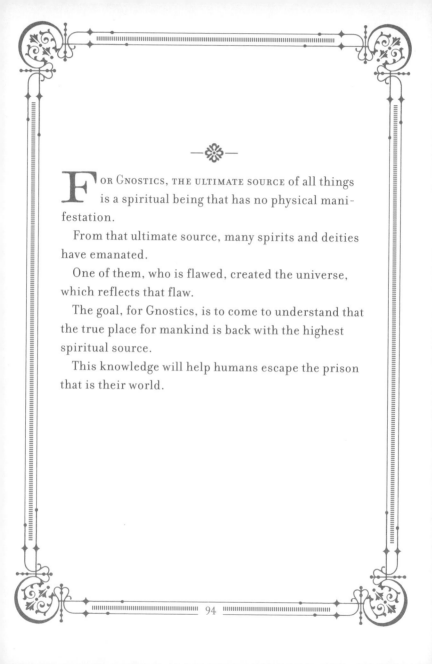

For Gnostics, the ultimate source of all things is a spiritual being that has no physical manifestation.

From that ultimate source, many spirits and deities have emanated.

One of them, who is flawed, created the universe, which reflects that flaw.

The goal, for Gnostics, is to come to understand that the true place for mankind is back with the highest spiritual source.

This knowledge will help humans escape the prison that is their world.

IN A 2010 POLL OF AMERICAN ADULTS conducted by the Pew Forum on Religion and Public Life, 82 percent knew that Mother Teresa was Catholic and 51 percent knew Joseph Smith was Mormon.

However, 53 percent of Protestants could not say who began the Reformation (Martin Luther), 45 percent of Catholics did not know that their Church teaches that the bread and wine in holy communion are *actually* (rather than *symbolically*) the body and blood of Christ, and 43 percent of Jews did not know that Maimonides (a leading philosopher and rabbinical authority) was Jewish.

POP QUIZ

The Juche Idea that "man is the master of everything and decides everything," has been called the state religion of what country?

a. China
b. North Korea
c. United States
d. Venezuela

ANSWER: b. North Korea

The word *juche* has been interpreted as "independent stand" and "spirit of self-reliance."

The Idea was articulated by Kim Il-Sung, the country's first Supreme Leader, and interpreted by his son and successor, Kim Jong-Il.

ONE OF THE CENTRAL TENETS OF JUDAISM is the belief in the coming of Mashiach, the anointed one.

According to scriptures, Mashiach will be a man, not a deity and not a savior.

He will be a skilled political and military leader, descendant of King David, who will return Jewish rule to Israel, which will become the center of all world government.

Under Mashiach, Jews who have been dispersed around the world will return to Israel, peace and prosperity will reign on earth, and all of humanity will recognize the Hebrew deity as the one, true God.

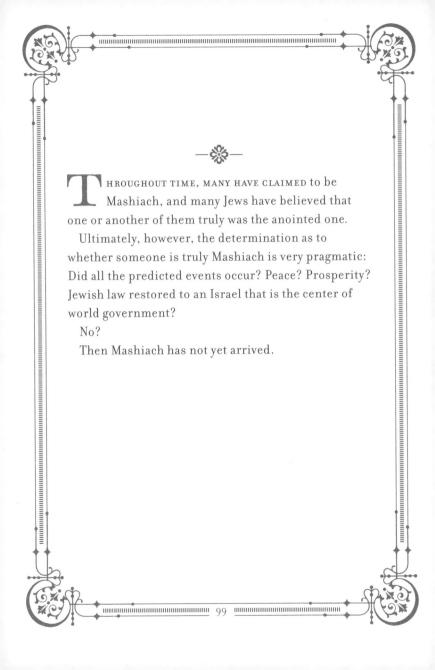

THROUGHOUT TIME, MANY HAVE CLAIMED to be Mashiach, and many Jews have believed that one or another of them truly was the anointed one.

Ultimately, however, the determination as to whether someone is truly Mashiach is very pragmatic: Did all the predicted events occur? Peace? Prosperity? Jewish law restored to an Israel that is the center of world government?

No?

Then Mashiach has not yet arrived.

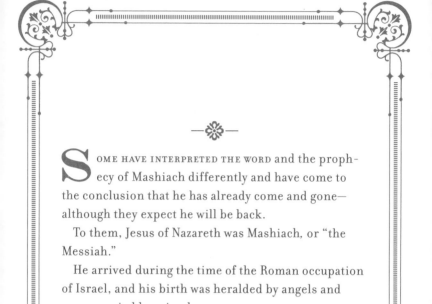

S OME HAVE INTERPRETED THE WORD and the prophecy of Mashiach differently and have come to the conclusion that he has already come and gone—although they expect he will be back.

To them, Jesus of Nazareth was Mashiach, or "the Messiah."

He arrived during the time of the Roman occupation of Israel, and his birth was heralded by angels and accompanied by miracles.

Jesus came in fulfillment of prophesy to deliver a message of a New Covenant between the Jews and God—essentially both to clarify and to alter the deal that God had made with His chosen people, the Israelites.

C HRIST," THE WORD OF GREEK and Latin derivation
for "messiah," has come to be synonymous with
Jesus, and his followers are known as Christians.

They believe that Jesus was God in human form, sent
to preach and then to be executed as part of a process
that would cleanse mankind of its sins.

His tale is told in a series of stories his followers see
as a supplement to the Jewish Bible, which they refer
to as the Old Testament.

The core of the story, called the New Testament, is
contained in four Gospels, stories told from the perspective of four of Jesus's disciples.

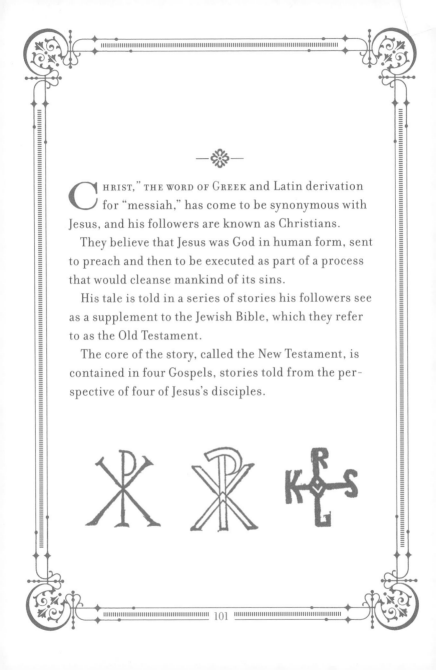

IN THE GOSPEL ACCORDING TO MATTHEW, Jesus provided many details of the New Covenant during his Sermon on the Mount.

One by one, he identified elements of the previous laws and reinterpreted them.

For example, he expanded the commandment against killing to include not only negative actions, but also negative thoughts: "…whoever is angry with his brother without a cause shall be in danger of the judgment."

He also expanded the commandment against adultery to include "whoever looks at a woman to lust for her" as an adulterer.

WHEN ASKED WHICH WAS THE greatest commandment in the law, according to the Gospel of Matthew (22:37-40), Jesus answered by condensing the 613 commandments in the Torah to two:

"'Thou shalt love the Lord thy God with all thy heart, and with all thy soul, and with all thy mind.'

"This is the first and great commandment.

"And the second is like unto it, Thou shalt love thy neighbor as thyself.

"On these two commandments hang all the law and the prophets."

"KADDISH" IS THE HEBREW PRAYER of mourning, but it does not mention death. Instead, it is a reaffirmation of faith in God.

A specific version of the kaddish is reserved for mourners hoping to help the soul of a parent purify itself before entering the World to Come (*Olam Ha-Ba*).

This process of purification can take as long as twelve months for those who were very evil.

To avoid the implication that the parent was *that* evil, a child is required to recite the kaddish daily for only eleven months, then annually on the anniversary of the parent's death.

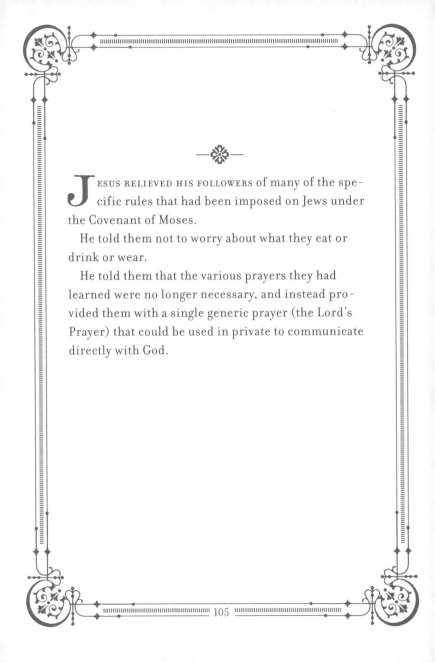

———— ❁ ————

JESUS RELIEVED HIS FOLLOWERS of many of the specific rules that had been imposed on Jews under the Covenant of Moses.

He told them not to worry about what they eat or drink or wear.

He told them that the various prayers they had learned were no longer necessary, and instead provided them with a single generic prayer (the Lord's Prayer) that could be used in private to communicate directly with God.

THE LORD'S PRAYER
(Catholic Version)

Our Father who art in heaven,
hallowed be thy name.

Thy kingdom come.

Thy will be done on Earth, as it is in heaven.

Give us this day our daily bread, and forgive us our trespasses, as we forgive those who trespass against us, and lead us not into temptation, but deliver us from evil.

THE LORD'S PRAYER
(King James Version)

Our Father which art in heaven, Hallowed be thy name.
Thy kingdom come, Thy will be done in Earth, as it is in heaven.

Give us this day our daily bread.

And forgive us our debts, as we forgive our debtors.
And lead us not into temptation, but deliver us from evil:

For thine is the kingdom, and the power, and the glory, forever.

Amen.

MATT. 6:9–13

A PRAYER FOR TOTAL FREEDOM

(The Church of Scientology)

May the author of the universe enable all men to reach an understanding of their spiritual nature.

May awareness and understanding of life expand, so that all may come to know the author of the universe.

And may others also reach this understanding which brings Total Freedom.

At this time, we think of those whose liberty is threatened; of those who have suffered imprisonment for their beliefs; of those who are enslaved or martyred, and for all those who are brutalized, trapped or attacked.

We pray that human rights will be preserved so that all people may believe and worship freely, so that freedom will once again be seen in our land.

Freedom from war, and poverty, and want; freedom to be; freedom to do and freedom to have.

Freedom to use and understand Man's potential—a potential that is God-given and Godlike.

And freedom to achieve that understanding and awareness that is Total Freedom.

May God let it be so.

MOST CHRISTIANS BELIEVE THAT, three days after Jesus was executed for his preachings, he rose from the dead and returned to walk and to preach among the people again.

His resurrection is celebrated as Easter, and he is said to have ascended to heaven under his own power forty days later.

Jesus promised to return, and Christians anticipate that time as the Second Coming, during which a period of utopian peace and prosperity will begin.

How are Jehovah's Witnesses different from traditional Christians?

One way is that Jehovah's Witnesses reject the notion of the Trinity (God, Jesus, and the Holy Spirit).

They believe that Jesus is the Son of God—God's first creation—but not a god himself.

Jesus was fully human and was killed to free mankind from sin and death.

Jesus was crucified on a single upright stake, rather than a cross, and was not resurrected in bodily form, but was raised from the dead as a spirit creature who returned to heaven.

Do Jehovah's Witnesses believe in an afterlife?

They believe that death brings an end to consciousness, but that someday soon, 144 thousand people will be taken to heaven to rule with God and Jesus over a paradise on Earth.

That paradise is coming soon, because the "end times" began in 1914, when Jesus was made King and banished Satan from heaven to Earth.

Do Jehovah's Witnesses celebrate Christmas?

No, they don't celebrate *anybody's* birthday. Birthdays (and most other holidays) are viewed as pagan celebrations.

The Bible, they say, does not call for celebrating any holiday other than the Memorial of Christ's Death.

That holiday is honored around the same time as Easter and Passover.

NEWS FLASH: Working for a Religious
Organization Is Not Likely to Lead to Wealth

According to the U.S. Bureau of Labor
Statistics, the average annual wage for people
working for religious organizations is $38,000, which
is slightly below the median American wage earner.

CEOs top the list with an average of more than
$130,000 per year, while "gaming service workers" are
at the bottom, earning only about $18,000 per year.

Most workers in the religious field fall under the
category of "community and social service occupa-
tions," and they make (on average) close to $42,000
per year.

ARLY IN THE SEVENTH CENTURY, a forty-year-old merchant named Muhammad ibn Abdallah began receiving revelations from God.

Muhammad's revelations, which make up the Quran, and an extensive record of his life, called the Hadith, are the two central documents at the core of Islam.

To followers of Islam, Muhammad is the last of a series of prophets to whom God has presented His message directly—beginning with Adam, and continuing with Abraham, Noah, David, Moses, and Jesus.

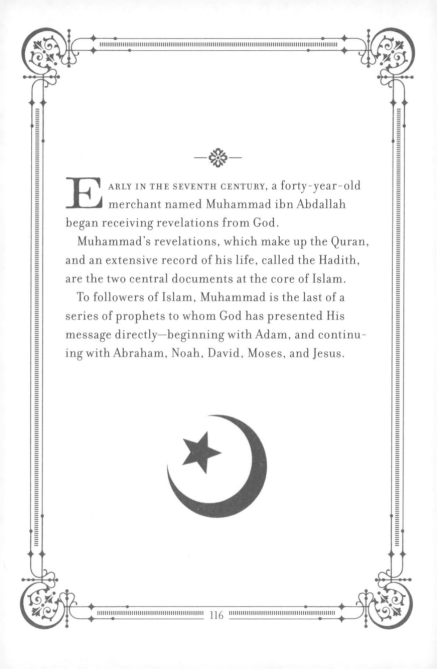

—❁—

In Islam, God is one—the immutable source of everything. This concept is called *tawhid,* and it is one of the fundamental tenets of this monotheistic religion.

God reveals His plans for humankind through divine revelation to prophets, such as the Torah of Moses and the Gospel of Jesus.

God chooses new prophets when the message is corrupted and needs to be restated.

IN ISLAM, THE NOTION OF THE TRINITY introduced in Christianity is considered to be in conflict with the idea that there is only one, true God.

The message God gave Muhammad to deliver as the Quran is considered the final, perfect version, and Muhammad is therefore considered the "seal" of prophecy.

Ultimately, when everything returns to its divine source as part of the Last Days, all people will be subjected to a Final Judgment based on how they answered the call of the prophets.

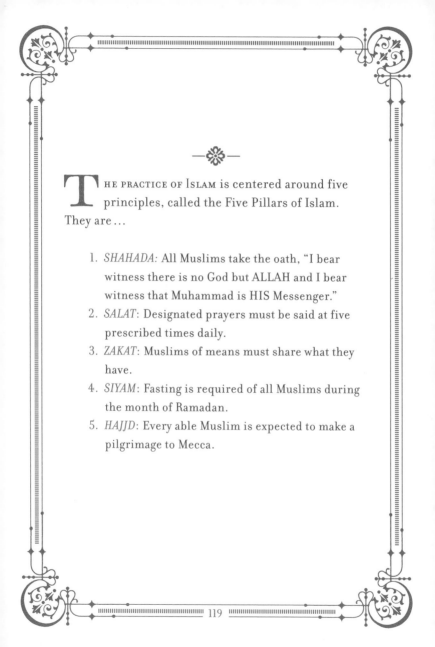

—❀—

THE PRACTICE OF ISLAM is centered around five principles, called the Five Pillars of Islam. They are …

1. *SHAHADA:* All Muslims take the oath, "I bear witness there is no God but ALLAH and I bear witness that Muhammad is HIS Messenger."
2. *SALAT:* Designated prayers must be said at five prescribed times daily.
3. *ZAKAT:* Muslims of means must share what they have.
4. *SIYAM:* Fasting is required of all Muslims during the month of Ramadan.
5. *HAJJD:* Every able Muslim is expected to make a pilgrimage to Mecca.

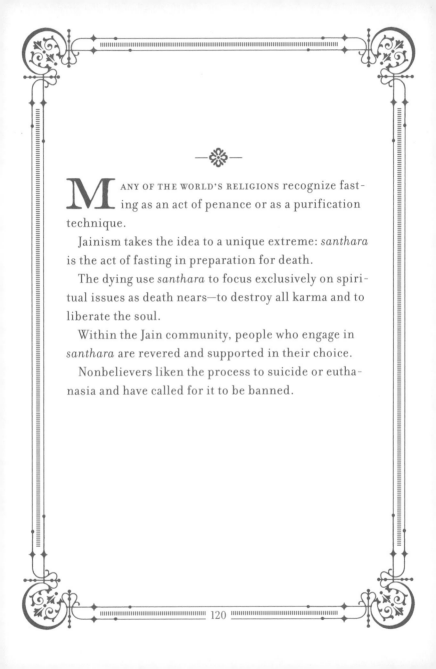

MANY OF THE WORLD'S RELIGIONS recognize fasting as an act of penance or as a purification technique.

Jainism takes the idea to a unique extreme: *santhara* is the act of fasting in preparation for death.

The dying use *santhara* to focus exclusively on spiritual issues as death nears—to destroy all karma and to liberate the soul.

Within the Jain community, people who engage in *santhara* are revered and supported in their choice.

Nonbelievers liken the process to suicide or euthanasia and have called for it to be banned.

THE TORAH CONTAINS THREE Tinjunctions against boiling a baby goat in its mother's milk.

That rule has been expanded through interpretation to prohibit any cooking of meat and dairy products together.

In fact, under the kosher dietary rules, not only can meat and dairy not be eaten together, two separate sets of cookware and tableware must be maintained—one exclusively for meat and the other exclusively for dairy.

A NIMALS THAT BOTH CHEW their cuds and have cloven hooves are considered fit to eat under kosher laws, but only if they have been killed in a particular ritualistic way: death must come quickly and as painlessly as possible, and all blood must be drained from the animal.

Birds of prey and insects are generally considered to be *treyf* (unclean, or not kosher).

To be kosher, a sea creature must have both fins and scales.

Food must satisfy many other rules of selection and preparation to be considered kosher.

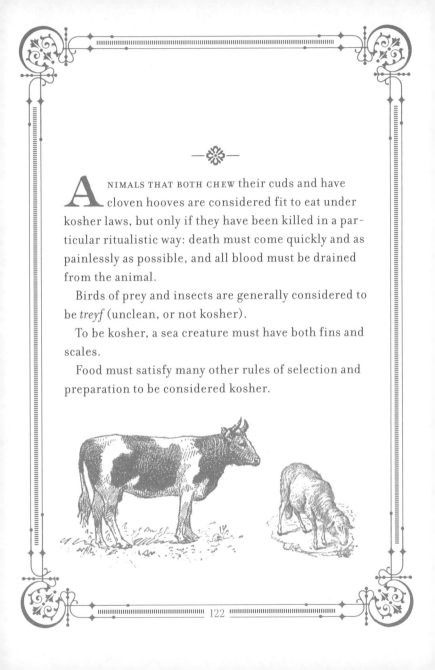

THE UNITARIAN UNIVERSALIST Association of
Congregations calls itself a "non-creedal"
faith, because it accepts people of a wide variety of
beliefs—including theists and atheists.

Formed by the merger of the Unitarians and the
Universalists in 1961, the Unitarian Universalists
promote the following seven principles:

1. Each person is important.
2. Be kind in all you do.
3. We're free to learn together.
4. We search for what is true.
5. All people need a voice.
6. Build a fair and peaceful world.
7. We care for the earth.

Do Buddhists believe in God?

Buddhism does not address issues of whether God exists, how the universe was created, or what the purpose of life might be.

Buddha dismissed such metaphysical questions as superfluous to the problem at hand—how to end suffering.

By analogy, he asked whether someone shot by a poison arrow would waste time wondering who shot the arrow, how the arrow was constructed, what kind of bow was used . . .

Instead, he suggested, the only important issue would be removing the arrow!

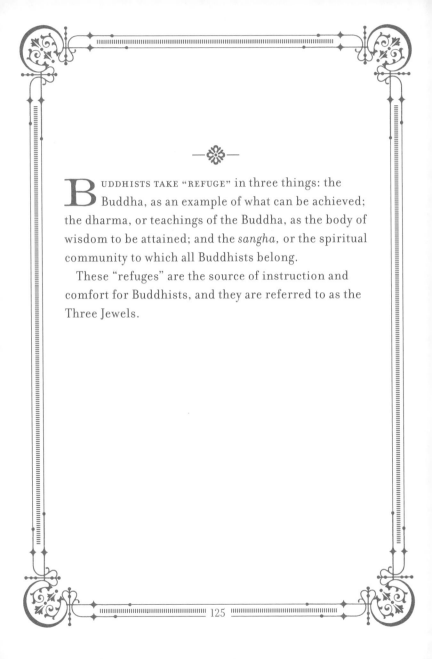

B UDDHISTS TAKE "REFUGE" in three things: the
Buddha, as an example of what can be achieved;
the dharma, or teachings of the Buddha, as the body of
wisdom to be attained; and the *sangha*, or the spiritual
community to which all Buddhists belong.

These "refuges" are the source of instruction and
comfort for Buddhists, and they are referred to as the
Three Jewels.

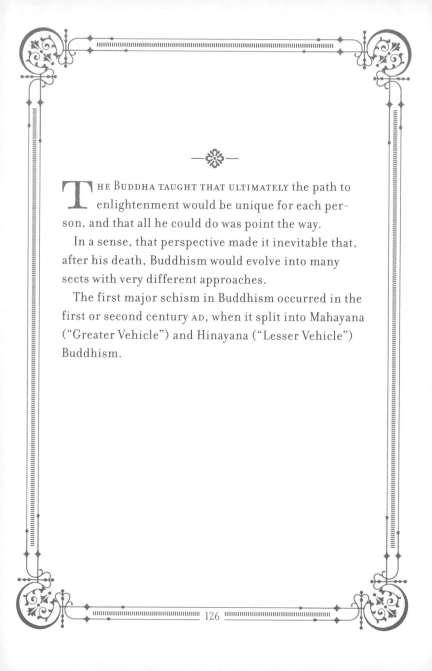

— ❀ —

T HE BUDDHA TAUGHT THAT ULTIMATELY the path to enlightenment would be unique for each person, and that all he could do was point the way.

In a sense, that perspective made it inevitable that, after his death, Buddhism would evolve into many sects with very different approaches.

The first major schism in Buddhism occurred in the first or second century AD, when it split into Mahayana ("Greater Vehicle") and Hinayana ("Lesser Vehicle") Buddhism.

In Mahayana Buddhism, enlightenment is thought to be accessible to everyone—not just monks—within a single lifetime.

An emphasis is placed on the "bodhisattva," an enlightened being who vows not to rest until *all* sentient beings reach enlightenment, and who is therefore available to help the devout.

Amitabha, for example, vowed that, when he became a buddha, he would create a paradise for those who had faith in him and called on him for help.

FOLLOWERS OF AMITABHA BUDDHA believe that enlightenment is not possible for most people without divine intervention.

Amitabha Buddha is worshipped as a savior who ensures that his followers are reborn in the Pure Land he created.

There, they can focus on attaining enlightenment with his help and without interruption or distraction.

THE PURE LAND SECT OF BUDDHISM began in India around the second century BC, spread to Eastern Asia, and evolved into one of the most popular sects of Buddhism in practice today.

With its emphasis on divine intervention to achieve liberation from samsara, the Pure Land sect has reincorporated some of the practices of Hinduism that Siddhartha Gautama originally rejected.

THE WORLD VALUES SURVEY polled the populations of thirty-eight countries on two related issues: Should religious people hold public office? Should religious leaders influence politics?

Denmark, Belgium, and France said religion and politics should stay separate, period.

In Romania and Malta, religious people could hold office, but religious leaders shouldn't influence politics. Sweden and the Netherlands went the other way.

The countries comfortable with religious influence going in both directions were the U.S., South Africa, Ukraine, Venezuela, Greece, and the Philippines.

C H'AN BUDDHISM, DEVELOPED IN CHINA in the sixth century BC, is also considered to be part of the Mahayana sect, but it has no emphasis on divine intervention.

Ch'an Buddhists (known as Zen Buddhists in Japan) believe that everyone has a Buddha nature, which can be brought out with the help of a teacher who oversees the student's meditation and study.

*In Tibetan Buddhism, how long is the
period between death and rebirth?*

a. It happens in an instant.

b. It depends on one's karma.

c. No one knows.

d. 49 days.

ANSWER: d. 49 days.

During the seven weeks it takes for a soul to be reborn, a Tibetan lama chants passages from the *Book of the Dead* to help the deceased either avoid rebirth or achieve a more positive rebirth.

THERAVADA BUDDHISM, sometimes considered part of Hinayana Buddhism, is considered the oldest form of the religion and the closest to the original teachings of Siddhartha Gautama.

In Theravada Buddhism, enlightenment can only be achieved through one's own efforts of meditation and concentration.

Theravada Buddhism rejects the notion of any supernatural assistance in liberation from samsara.

This form of Buddhism is popular in southern Asia.

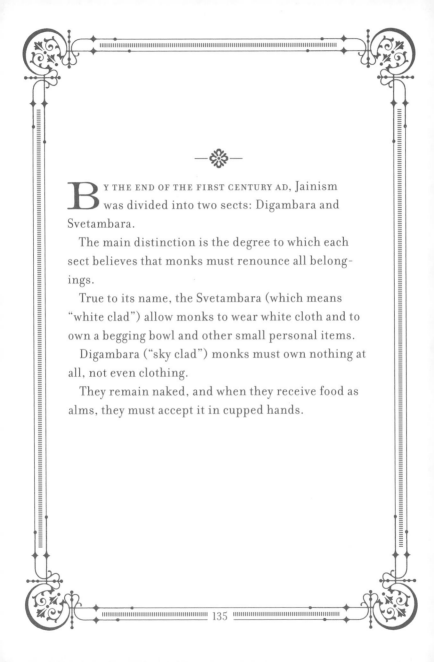

B Y THE END OF THE FIRST CENTURY AD, Jainism was divided into two sects: Digambara and Svetambara.

The main distinction is the degree to which each sect believes that monks must renounce all belongings.

True to its name, the Svetambara (which means "white clad") allow monks to wear white cloth and to own a begging bowl and other small personal items.

Digambara ("sky clad") monks must own nothing at all, not even clothing.

They remain naked, and when they receive food as alms, they must accept it in cupped hands.

THE SVETAMBARA JAINS AND the Digambara Jains also differ significantly in their outlook on women.

The Digambara believe that women cannot achieve enlightenment, but must instead be reborn as men.

The Svetambara not only think women can achieve enlightenment, they believe that Malli, the nineteenth *tirthankara* (literally, "ford-maker"), was a woman.

The Digambara disagree, insisting that Malli was a man.

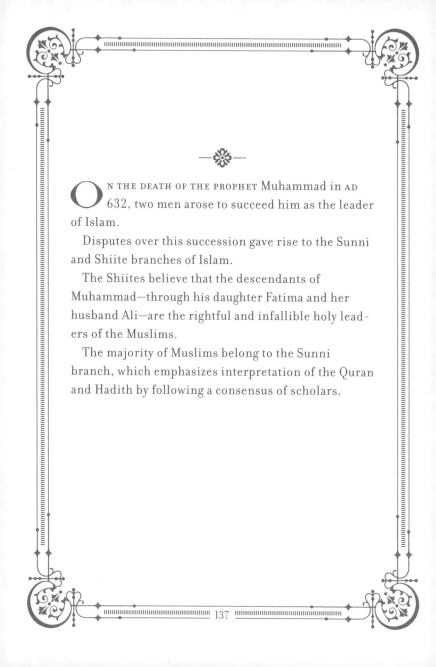

ON THE DEATH OF THE PROPHET Muhammad in AD 632, two men arose to succeed him as the leader of Islam.

Disputes over this succession gave rise to the Sunni and Shiite branches of Islam.

The Shiites believe that the descendants of Muhammad—through his daughter Fatima and her husband Ali—are the rightful and infallible holy leaders of the Muslims.

The majority of Muslims belong to the Sunni branch, which emphasizes interpretation of the Quran and Hadith by following a consensus of scholars.

THE MAJORITY OF SHIITES BELIEVE that there have been fourteen infallible leaders—Muhammad; his daughter, Fatima; and the twelve imams who succeeded Muhammad, beginning with Fatima's husband, Ali.

The Twelvers, as they are called, believe that Muhammad ibn al-Hasan, the twelfth imam, did not die.

He was born in AD 869 and became imam upon the death of his father in AD 874.

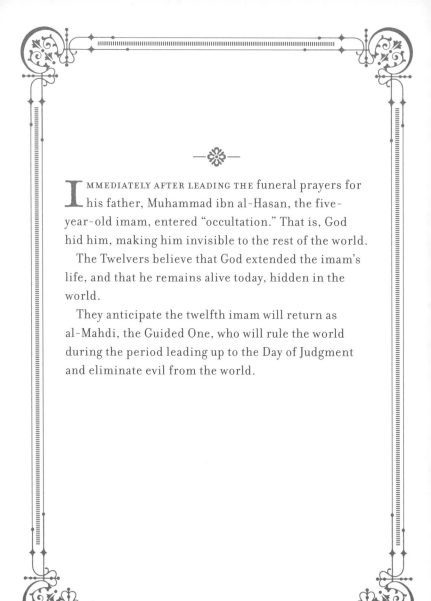

IMMEDIATELY AFTER LEADING THE funeral prayers for his father, Muhammad ibn al-Hasan, the five-year-old imam, entered "occultation." That is, God hid him, making him invisible to the rest of the world.

The Twelvers believe that God extended the imam's life, and that he remains alive today, hidden in the world.

They anticipate the twelfth imam will return as al-Mahdi, the Guided One, who will rule the world during the period leading up to the Day of Judgment and eliminate evil from the world.

THE U.S. COMMISSION ON INTERNATIONAL Religious Freedom is an independent agency created by Congress, and each year it releases a list of "countries of particular concern" (CPCs) with regard to violations of freedom of religion.

Here are the fifteen countries that made the list in 2013: Burma,* China,* Egypt, Eritrea,* Iran,* Iraq, Nigeria, North Korea,* Pakistan, Saudi Arabia,* Sudan,* Tajikistan, Turkmenistan, Uzbekistan,* and Vietnam.

(*Those countries with an asterisk were also cited by the State Department as CPCs.)

Long after the ancient nations of Judah and Israel fell, and long before the Israel of today was conceived, a Jewish nation thrived in eastern Europe.

In the early ninth century, the Khazars occupied the land from the northern shores of the Black Sea, east to the northern shores of the Caspian Sea—in what is now Ukraine.

At that time, the king of the Khazars is said to have held a debate among representatives of the Christian, Jewish, and Muslim faiths.

When it was over, the rulers adopted Judaism as their national religion and converted.

THE JEWISH NATION OF KHAZARIA flourished for more than 100 years.

Synagogues and Jewish schools were established.

The people learned to speak and to write in Hebrew, and they studied the Torah.

In 860, Saint Cyril is said to have attempted in vain to convert the Khazars to Christianity, but they remained a Jewish people until they were conquered, in the tenth century, by the Russians.

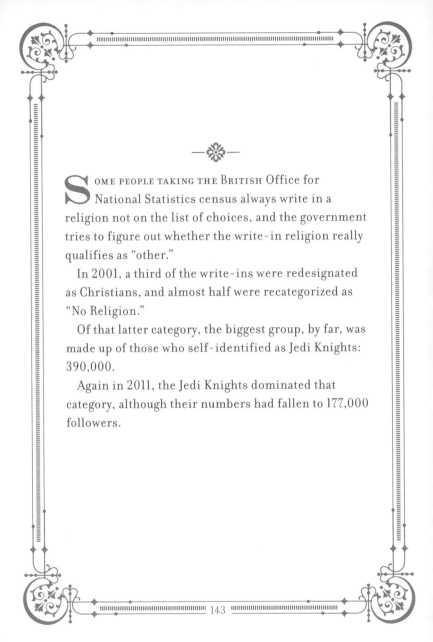

SOME PEOPLE TAKING THE BRITISH Office for National Statistics census always write in a religion not on the list of choices, and the government tries to figure out whether the write-in religion really qualifies as "other."

In 2001, a third of the write-ins were redesignated as Christians, and almost half were recategorized as "No Religion."

Of that latter category, the biggest group, by far, was made up of those who self-identified as Jedi Knights: 390,000.

Again in 2011, the Jedi Knights dominated that category, although their numbers had fallen to 177,000 followers.

THE ADULT POPULATION OF THE U.S. increased by about 30 percent from 1990 to 2008, according to the American Religious Identification Survey.

Using open-ended questions, the survey asked how people self-identify their religion.

The chart on the opposite page shows how the religious makeup of the population changed in that time:

RELIGOUS MAKEUP OF THE U.S.

	1990	2008	+/-
	In thousands		*Percent*
ALL ADULTS	175,440	207,983	+30%
CHRISTIANITY	151,225	173,402	+15%
JUDAISM	3,137	2,680	−15%
ISLAM	527	1,349	+156%
BUDDHISM	404	1,189	+194%
NO RELIGION	14,331	34,169	+138%
REFUSED TO SAY	4,031	11,815	+193%

For a thousand years after the death of Jesus, his followers were members of a unified church.

In 1054, the first big schism in Christianity occurred, separating the Catholics from the Eastern Orthodox.

About 500 years later, Martin Luther further split the church by challenging the position of the Catholic Pope as the only human in direct communion with God.

Today, there are hundreds of so-called Protestant sects of Christianity.

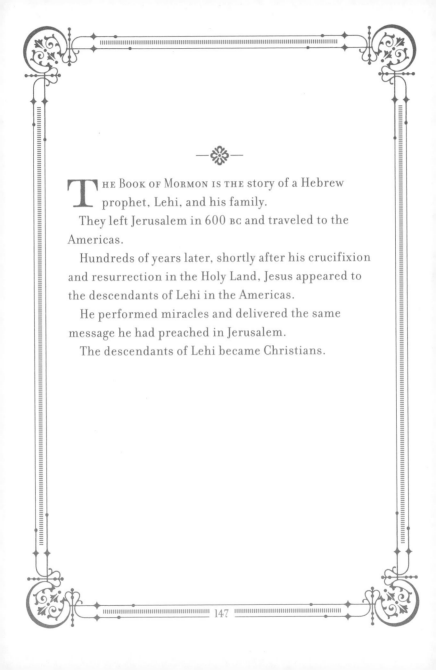

THE BOOK OF MORMON IS THE story of a Hebrew prophet, Lehi, and his family.

They left Jerusalem in 600 BC and traveled to the Americas.

Hundreds of years later, shortly after his crucifixion and resurrection in the Holy Land, Jesus appeared to the descendants of Lehi in the Americas.

He performed miracles and delivered the same message he had preached in Jerusalem.

The descendants of Lehi became Christians.

THREE HUNDRED YEARS AFTER Jesus appeared in the Americas, as the last of the first American Christians were dying off, a prophet named Mormon recorded the history of his people on a set of golden plates and hid them.

In 1827, in a town in upstate New York, Joseph Smith was led to discover those golden plates left behind by Mormon.

Smith translated those plates, which became the *Book of Mormon,* another testament to the story of Jesus as the messiah and savior.

SMITH STARTED A SMALL CONGREGATION known as the Church of Jesus Christ of Latter-day Saints, but he met with consistent rejection and persecution.

He and his followers were forced to flee westward, stopping first in Missouri, then continuing on until the group known today as Mormons settled in Utah.

More than 100 million copies of the *Book of Mormon* have been published in more than ninety-three languages, and more than 50,000 missionaries are delivering the story of the church to 162 countries around the world.

THE MORMONS PROFESS thirteen Articles of Faith, the first of which is belief in the Trinity—God, Jesus, and the Holy Ghost.

The second disavows the notion of Original Sin—that all humans bear responsibility for the disobedience of Adam and Eve.

Mormons also profess belief that the tribes of ancient Israel will be restored, and that the New Jerusalem (Zion) will be built on the American continent.

The thirteenth Article says, "If there is anything virtuous, lovely, or of good report or praiseworthy, we seek after these things."

MORMONS CONSIDER free will to be a gift from God.

Since addiction can compromise free will, any substance that is generally addictive is considered improper.

For that reason, in addition to the general belief that God wants people to maintain their own physical health, Mormons are told not to drink alcohol, not to use tobacco, and not to ingest caffeine.

Even addictive prescription drugs are to be taken with caution.

*Which religion has the following as its
first-stated aim?*

"A civilization without insanity, without criminals and
without war, where the able can prosper and honest
beings can have rights, and where Man is free to rise to
greater heights . . ."

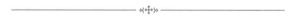

The Church of Scientology

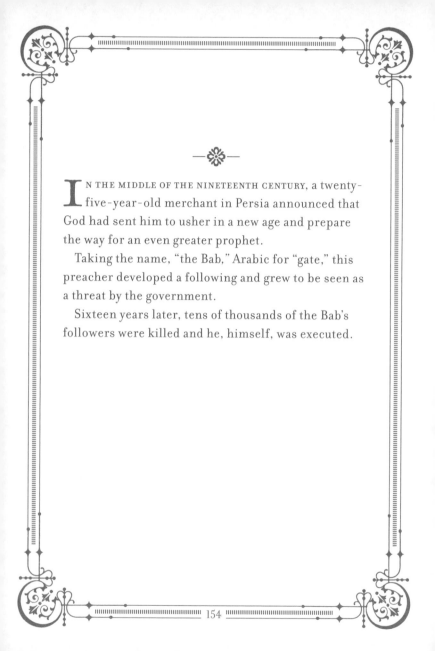

IN THE MIDDLE OF THE NINETEENTH CENTURY, a twenty-five-year-old merchant in Persia announced that God had sent him to usher in a new age and prepare the way for an even greater prophet.

Taking the name, "the Bab," Arabic for "gate," this preacher developed a following and grew to be seen as a threat by the government.

Sixteen years later, tens of thousands of the Bab's followers were killed and he, himself, was executed.

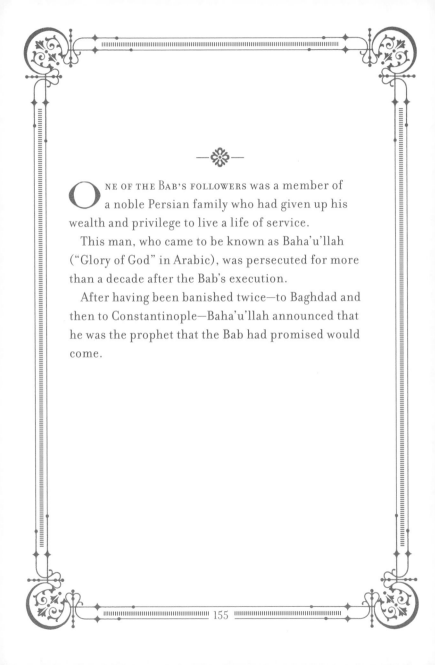

—❀—

ONE OF THE BAB'S FOLLOWERS was a member of a noble Persian family who had given up his wealth and privilege to live a life of service.

This man, who came to be known as Baha'u'llah ("Glory of God" in Arabic), was persecuted for more than a decade after the Bab's execution.

After having been banished twice—to Baghdad and then to Constantinople—Baha'u'llah announced that he was the prophet that the Bab had promised would come.

From 1863 to 1892, Baha'u'llah outlined his new religion in a series of scriptures and established the laws and institutions of the faith that has come to be known as Baha'i.

When he died in 1892, Baha'u'llah named his son as his successor.

The following year, the Baha'i faith was acknowledged in Chicago at the first Parliament of the World's Religions.

IN THE 20TH CENTURY, the mantle of leadership of the Baha'i faith was passed to Shoghi Effendi, the great-grandson of Baha'u'llah.

Shoghi Effendi helped grow the faith into a world-wide religion, with more than 5 million members around the globe.

The governing body of the Baha'i faith is the Universal House of Justice, whose members are elected every five years.

The message of Baha'u'llah (baha'i)

- The human race is ready to be unified into a grand society.
- All world religions have a common origin and a unity of purpose.
- Science and religion are not in conflict, but reflect complementary aspects of reality.
- Men and women are equal and all forms of prejudice should be eliminated.
- Spirituality offers a solution to economic problems.
- A federation of nations should be formed to establish a peaceful world commonwealth.

THE BAHA'I RECOGNIZE THE writings of Baha'u'llah as the most sacred texts.

He wrote thousands of documents, including letters to all of the world rulers of his day.

In those letters, Baha'u'llah warned of the catastrophic events that awaited the world if the rulers did not act in unison to establish a world order of peace and justice.

In addition to the writings of Baha'u'llah, the Baha'i also recognize the writings of the Bab, the Quran, the Old and New Testaments, and all the sacred writings of Buddhism, Hinduism, and Zoroastrianism as divine scripture.

*Are murder rates higher in religious nations
or secular nations?*

The more religious countries—the ones with deeper and more widespread belief in God throughout their populations—have higher murder rates.

In fact, even within the U.S., the more religious states are also the states with the highest rates of murder and violent crime.

MANY OF THE FOUNDING FATHERS of the U.S. held themselves to be deists—believers in God, but not necessarily in any of the organized religions of their day.

Deism focuses on reason and science, eschewing faith as a basis for belief.

Deists see evidence of the existence of God in nature and in the fact that living beings have a consciousness.

They tend to view God as the first cause—in essence, the answer to the chicken/egg question.

DEISM DIFFERENTIATES ITSELF from other religions by referring to them as "revealed religions"—that is, they are based on scriptures that were provided as revelations from God to specific individuals.

Deists consider the revealed religions to be based on greed and fear.

The promise of eternal life, or that requests made through prayer will be granted, appeals to greed.

Concerns about being judged at death for things done during life are motivated by fear of punishment.

*T*he *Age of Reason*, WRITTEN BY THOMAS PAINE, has become a deistic credo.

In it, Paine explains that religions claiming to be based on revelation are actually built on hearsay.

That is, the revelations of religions such as Judaism, Christianity, and Islam were made to only one person, then communicated to the rest of the world by word of mouth (and only later written down).

—❖—

HERE ARE SOME RECOGNIZABLE NAMES that some deists today consider among their antecedents:

- → Neil Armstrong
- → Leonardo da Vinci
- → Thomas Edison
- → Benjamin Franklin
- → Thomas Jefferson
- → Isaac Newton
- → Thomas Paine
- → Mark Twain
- → Voltaire
- → George Washington

CaoDai is a faith formed in 1926 in Vietnam, and it maintains that all religions have the same divine origin—whether it is called God, Allah, or the Tao.

In CaoDai, the truth is the same in all religions, and they are all founded on an ethic of love and justice.

Accordingly, "God and humans are one. Humans shall observe love and justice in order to be unified with God."

Although originally suppressed by the Communist government of Vietnam, CaoDai gained state recognition in 1997.

POP QUIZ

In CaoDai, the pantheon of saints includes which of the following people?

a. William Shakespeare
b. Victor Hugo
c. Vladimir Lenin
d. Louis Pasteur

A N S W E R : All of them.

All four famous westerners are considered saints, along with Moses, Jesus, Muhammad, and Joan of Arc.

*What is the ceremony surrounding
circumcision for Hebrews about?*

A Jewish boy is accepted into the religious community at
the age of eight days with the ritual act of circumcision,
called a *brit milah*.

The circumcision, conducted by a specialist ("mohel"),
is considered the completion of the body in keeping with
the instructions of God.

Parents wait until after the circumcision to name the
child, which is done as part of the ceremony.

Do Muslims get circumcised too?

In Islam, boys are routinely circumcised at the age of ten (or when they can recite the Quran).

Female circumcision is a controversial practice in the Muslim world.

Some countries have outlawed it, but it continues in others.

Many Islamic scholars say female circumcision has no basis in the Quran or the Hadith.

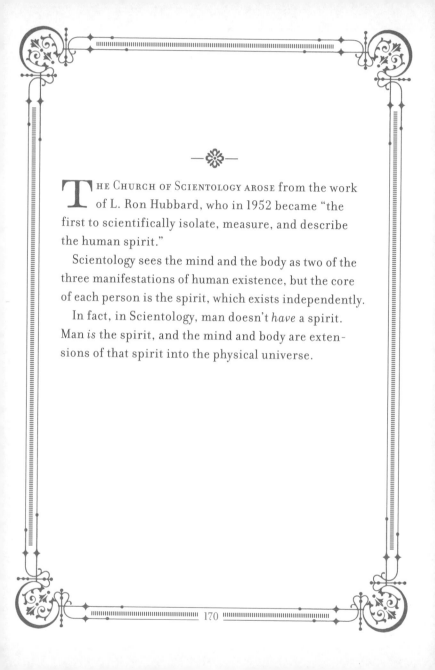

THE CHURCH OF SCIENTOLOGY AROSE from the work of L. Ron Hubbard, who in 1952 became "the first to scientifically isolate, measure, and describe the human spirit."

Scientology sees the mind and the body as two of the three manifestations of human existence, but the core of each person is the spirit, which exists independently.

In fact, in Scientology, man doesn't *have* a spirit. Man *is* the spirit, and the mind and body are extensions of that spirit into the physical universe.

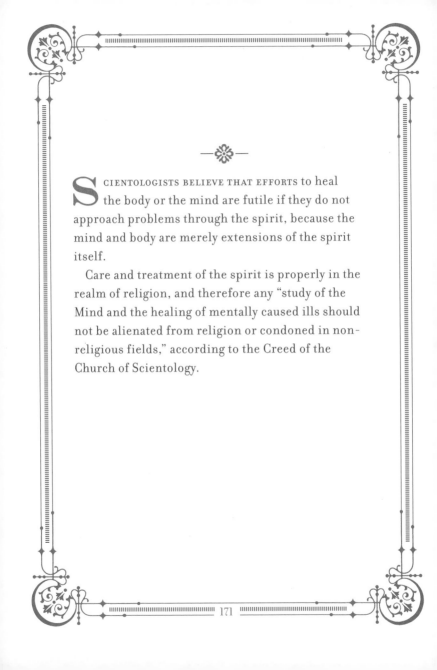

SCIENTOLOGISTS BELIEVE THAT EFFORTS to heal the body or the mind are futile if they do not approach problems through the spirit, because the mind and body are merely extensions of the spirit itself.

Care and treatment of the spirit is properly in the realm of religion, and therefore any "study of the Mind and the healing of mentally caused ills should not be alienated from religion or condoned in non-religious fields," according to the Creed of the Church of Scientology.

S CIENTOLOGISTS BELIEVE THAT THE fundamental
command followed by all living creatures is
"Survive!"

By analyzing the drives (Dynamics) associated with
that mandate for survival, Scientology hopes to focus
our understanding of ourselves, what motivates us,
and what it will take to bring those forces into har-
mony to improve our existence.

SCIENTOLOGY'S EIGHT DYNAMICS

1. SELF: the drive to survive as an individual—mind and body, as well as possessions—for as long as possible.
2. CREATIVITY: the drive to make things for the future, including children and a family.
3. GROUP SURVIVAL: the drive to form social structures—communities, companies, clubs, governments—through which one survives.
4. SPECIES: the drive to ensure that the species of humankind continues to survive.
5. LIFE-FORMS: the drive to survive as a life-form, in conjunction with other life-forms.
6. PHYSICAL UNIVERSE: the drive of the entire physical universe—space, time, matter, and energy—to survive.
7. SPIRITUAL DYNAMIC: the drive for the life force to survive on a more esoteric plane, such as through ideas or concepts.
8. INFINITE EXISTENCE: the drive of the infinite unity of being—commonly called God—to survive.

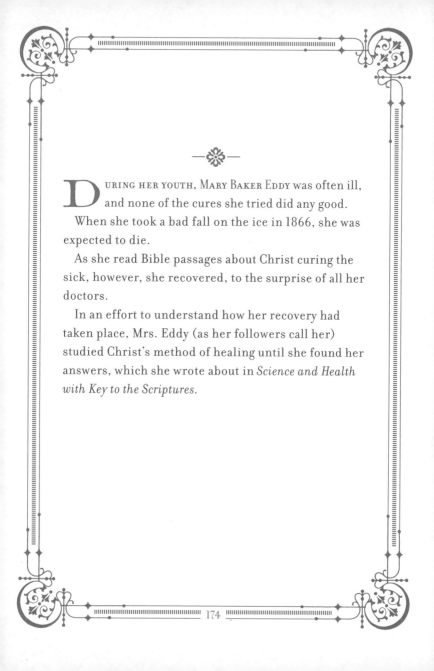

During her youth, Mary Baker Eddy was often ill, and none of the cures she tried did any good.

When she took a bad fall on the ice in 1866, she was expected to die.

As she read Bible passages about Christ curing the sick, however, she recovered, to the surprise of all her doctors.

In an effort to understand how her recovery had taken place, Mrs. Eddy (as her followers call her) studied Christ's method of healing until she found her answers, which she wrote about in *Science and Health with Key to the Scriptures.*

IN 1879, MRS. EDDY FOUNDED THE First Church of Christ, Scientist.

The pastor of the Church is two books: the Bible and Mrs. Eddy's *Science and Health*.

Every Sunday, Christian Scientists meet to read a Bible Lesson on a topic that members around the world have been studying all week long.

There are also midweek meetings during which members share stories about healing through the practice of Christian Science.

FUNDAMENTALLY, CHRISTIAN SCIENTISTS believe that our physical existence—including sin and ill health—are not real.

The goal is to attain a "spiritual understanding that casts out evil as unreal."

The belief that this life and physical existence are real is what makes illness possible.

An understanding of the spiritual nature of existence should eliminate illness.

Unlike other Christian faiths, in which sin is said to be punished by God, Christian Science teaches that it is the *belief in sin* that is punished, and that the punishment will stop when the belief in sin ends.

For many Christians, The Apostles' Creed is a succinct summary of the core beliefs of their religion.

- I believe in God, the Father almighty, creator of heaven and earth.
- I believe in Jesus Christ, his only Son, our Lord.
- He was conceived by the power of the Holy Spirit and born of the Virgin Mary.
- He suffered under Pontius Pilate, was crucified, died, and was buried.
- He descended into hell.
- On the third day he rose again.
- He ascended into heaven and is seated at the right hand of the Father.
- He will come again to judge the living and the dead.
- I believe in the Holy Spirit, the holy catholic Church, the communion of saints, the forgiveness of sins, the resurrection of the body, and the life everlasting.

WHEN IT COMES TO RELIGION IN THE U.S., there are some very strong correlations with age, geography, and political affiliation.

According to the 2012 General Social Survey, 40 percent of liberals said they had no religious preference versus 9 percent of conservatives.

Similarly, a third of Americans aged eighteen to twenty-four years old said "no preference" versus 7 percent in the seventy-five-and-over crowd.

Regionally, the Northeast and the West Coast were most likely to say none, while Midwesterners and Southerners were least likely.

T HE ISLAMIC CALENDAR IS BASED on the lunar cycle, so it falls behind the solar year by about eleven days each year.

Therefore, over the course of about thirty-two years, any particular date on the calendar will occur during all the seasons.

The last month of the Islamic year, Dhu al-Hijja, is when pilgrims are expected to go on their hajj (pilgrimage to Mecca).

The two great feast days of the year occur at the end of the fast of Ramadan and at the time of the hajj.

POP QUIZ

What is the largest religious gathering on Earth?

a. The Islamic pilgrimage to Mecca
b. The Hindu gathering in the River Ganges
c. The Burning Man festival in the Southwest U.S.
d. The papal address on Christmas Eve in Rome

ANSWER: b.

The Kumbh Mela is held every twelve years in Allahabad, India. In 2013, more than 120 million people gathered over a period of fifty-five days to bathe in the holy waters of the "Sangam"—the place where the Ganga, Yamuna, and (the mythical) Saraswati Rivers join.

What is the holiest site of the Sikhs?

The Harmandir Sashib (Golden Temple) is in Amritsar, India. Built in the late sixteenth century, the Temple is still an active place of worship and a frequent destination of Sikh pilgrims.

It is also open to the public. Every day, free meals are offered by temple volunteers to 35,000 people in the traditional dining hall.

THE ALLIANCE OF RELIGION and Conservation
estimates that 155 million pilgrimages take
place each year to the top thirty-two destinations
alone. Here are some of the most popular:

- → Ayyappan Saranam (Hindu)
    Sabarimala, India
    30 million pilgrims
- → Our Lady of Guadalupe Basilica (Christian)
    Mexico City
    20 million pilgrims
- → The Golden Temple (Sikh)
    Amritsar, India
    13 million pilgrims
- → Husayn Mosque (Muslim)
    Karbala, Iraq
    10 million pilgrims
- → Western (Wailing) Wall (Judaism)
    Jerusalem, Israel
    8 million pilgrims
- → Wutai Shan (Taoist)
    Shanxi, China
    2.1 million pilgrims

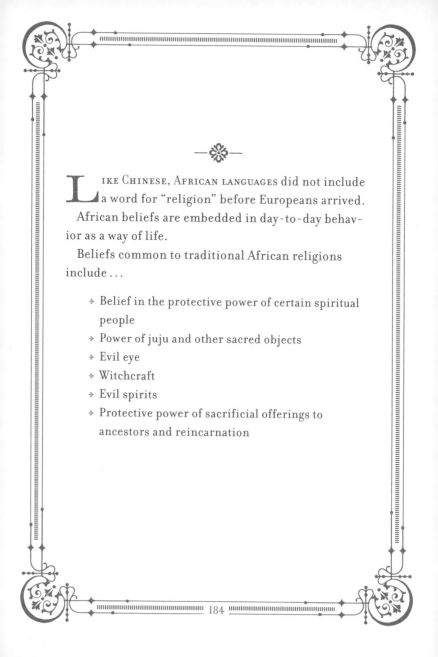

L IKE CHINESE, AFRICAN LANGUAGES did not include a word for "religion" before Europeans arrived. African beliefs are embedded in day-to-day behavior as a way of life.

Beliefs common to traditional African religions include . . .

- → Belief in the protective power of certain spiritual people
- → Power of juju and other sacred objects
- → Evil eye
- → Witchcraft
- → Evil spirits
- → Protective power of sacrificial offerings to ancestors and reincarnation

W HEN CULTURES COLLIDE, their religious ideas tend to merge and coalesce into a new form of worship.

This process is called "syncretism," and it is what happened when slaves were brought from Africa to the New World.

In Brazil, the combination of African religions and Catholicism gave birth to Candomble, a polytheistic religion that incorporates music and dance in a ceremony to summon spirits, or *oriashas*.

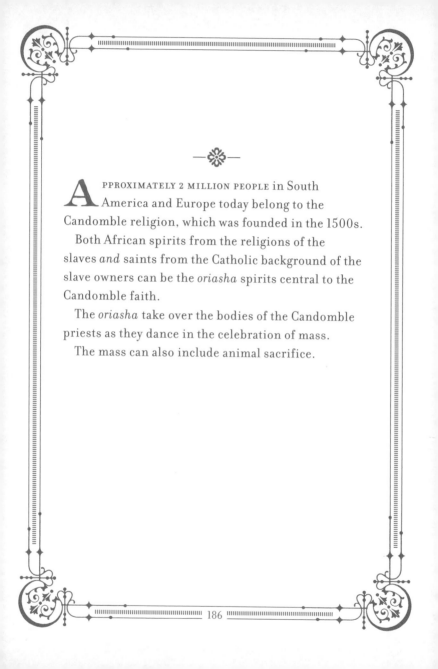

APPROXIMATELY 2 MILLION PEOPLE in South America and Europe today belong to the Candomble religion, which was founded in the 1500s.

Both African spirits from the religions of the slaves *and* saints from the Catholic background of the slave owners can be the *oriasha* spirits central to the Candomble faith.

The *oriasha* take over the bodies of the Candomble priests as they dance in the celebration of mass.

The mass can also include animal sacrifice.

SANTERIA IS A SYNCRETIC RELIGION that combines Roman Catholic traditions of Cuba with Yoruba beliefs from Africa.

In Santeria, the main deity, Olodumare, has a destiny planned for each person at birth.

To complete that destiny, the follower must engage in rituals worshipping "orishas," which are mortal spirit-manifestations of Olodumare who must be worshipped to survive.

That makes the relationship between orishas and humans a mutually beneficial one.

Is voodoo a religion?

Voodoo is a melding of various African religious practices with some aspects of Christianity (especially Roman Catholicism).

In Louisiana, voodoo is the product of the French, Spanish, and Creole peoples who lived there.

Haitian voodoo is a product of the Catholic practices of the French colonists and the African influences of the slaves they brought with them.

THE IMAM REZA SHRINE (Mashhad, Iran) is named after the eighth imam of Twelver Shiites. It is said to be the largest mosque in the world, by dimension.

The Al-Masjid Al-Haram in Mecca, Saudi Arabia, is the largest mosque by capacity, with room for 2 million worshippers.

The Belz Great Synagogue in Jerusalem is the largest in the world, with room for 6,000 worshippers and a record-breaking ark capable of housing seventy Torah scrolls.

S t. Peter's Basilica in Vatican City is the largest Roman Catholic church in the world, with an interior volume of 1.2 million cubic meters.

The claim of largest Anglican/Episcopal cathedral is in dispute, claimed by both the unfinished Cathedral of St. John the Divine in New York City, and by the Liverpool Cathedral in England.

T HE TEMPLES OF ANGKOR COMPRISE what is considered the largest religious complex in the world.

Built during the Khmer Empire (from the ninth to the fourteenth centuries), they cover more than 150 square miles in the Cambodian province of Siem Reap.

Temples include Angkor Wat, the Bayon, Preah Khan, and Ta Prohm.

Over the history of the region, Hinduism and Buddhism were alternately practiced at those temples, depending on who was in charge at the time.

F ROM 1991 TO 2011, THE PERCENTAGE OF U.S. adults who said they "accept Jesus and expect to be saved" rose from 35 percent to 40 percent, according to a poll by Barna Group.

That 20-year trend is belied by many of the other statistics that came out of the same poll.

20-YEAR TRENDS

	1991	2011
READ BIBLE OUTSIDE CHURCH	45%	40%
VOLUNTEERED AT CHURCH	27%	19%
ATTEND ADULT SUNDAY SCHOOL	23%	15%
ATTEND WORSHIP	49%	40%
CALL THE BIBLE "TOTALLY ACCURATE" IN ALL PRINCIPLES	46%	38%
DEFINE GOD AS ALL-KNOWING, ALL-POWERFUL RULER	74%	67%

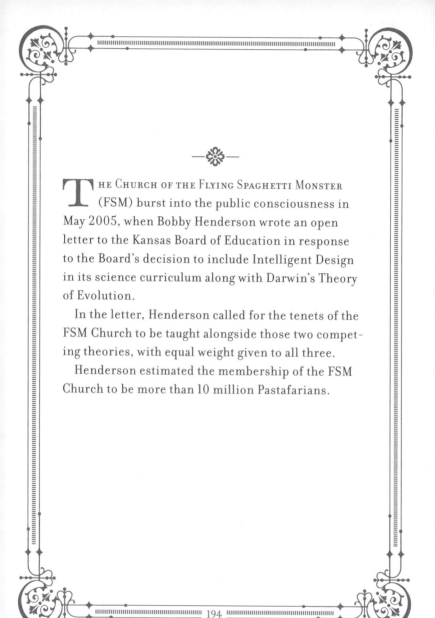

THE CHURCH OF THE FLYING SPAGHETTI MONSTER (FSM) burst into the public consciousness in May 2005, when Bobby Henderson wrote an open letter to the Kansas Board of Education in response to the Board's decision to include Intelligent Design in its science curriculum along with Darwin's Theory of Evolution.

In the letter, Henderson called for the tenets of the FSM Church to be taught alongside those two competing theories, with equal weight given to all three.

Henderson estimated the membership of the FSM Church to be more than 10 million Pastafarians.

T HE FSM Church doctrine holds that the Flying
Spaghetti Monster created the earth, intention-
ally making it appear to be older than it is.

Whenever tests are conducted, such as carbon-
dating, to determine the age of the world, the Flying
Spaghetti Monster is believed to be standing by, alter-
ing the measurements with His noodly appendages.

The Church also maintains that, because the tem-
perature of the world appears to have climbed as the
number of pirates worldwide has decreased, the solution to Global Warming is for more people to become
pirates.

WHEN A MEMBER OF THE FSM Church in Austria went to renew his driver's license in 2011, he insisted on wearing the appropriate religious head-gear (a colander) when his picture was taken.

The government of Austria apparently consented, and the episode made news around the world.

Two years later, in New Jersey, a similar request by a Pastafarian was denied.

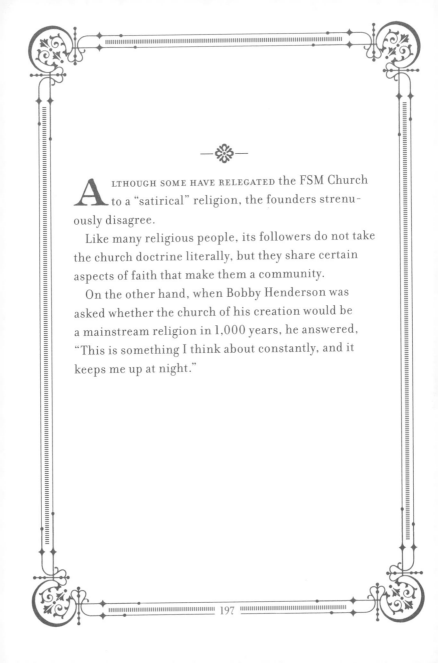

ALTHOUGH SOME HAVE RELEGATED the FSM Church to a "satirical" religion, the founders strenuously disagree.

Like many religious people, its followers do not take the church doctrine literally, but they share certain aspects of faith that make them a community.

On the other hand, when Bobby Henderson was asked whether the church of his creation would be a mainstream religion in 1,000 years, he answered, "This is something I think about constantly, and it keeps me up at night."

IN THE BEGINNING, THERE WAS THE DREAMTIME—
according to the aboriginal peoples of Australia.

The world was flat and barren, and supernatural beings roamed the land.

Known as the creative ancestors, those beings gave rise to all living creatures and the landscape.

Some of them turned into rocks and watering holes and other specific landmarks.

To the aboriginal peoples, the land itself has a spiritual value, and places where those creative ancestors "settled" are considered even more holy.

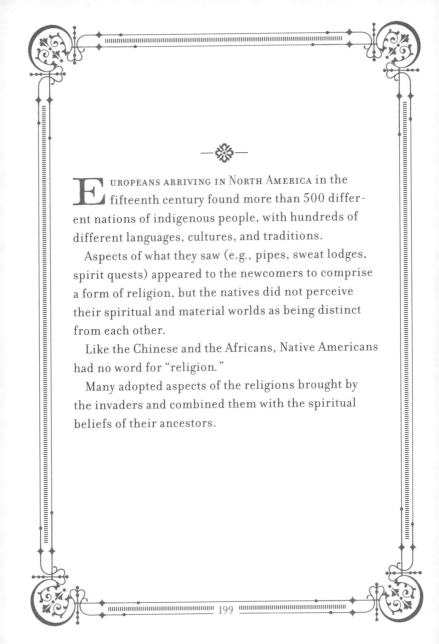

EUROPEANS ARRIVING IN NORTH AMERICA in the fifteenth century found more than 500 different nations of indigenous people, with hundreds of different languages, cultures, and traditions.

Aspects of what they saw (e.g., pipes, sweat lodges, spirit quests) appeared to the newcomers to comprise a form of religion, but the natives did not perceive their spiritual and material worlds as being distinct from each other.

Like the Chinese and the Africans, Native Americans had no word for "religion."

Many adopted aspects of the religions brought by the invaders and combined them with the spiritual beliefs of their ancestors.

What does the word "Shinto" mean?

Shinto, the common name for Japan's indigenous religion, is a combination of the Chinese symbols *shen* ("spirit") and tao ("way").

Before the arrival of the Chinese, the Japanese had called the religion "Kami no Michi" (the Way of the Gods).

The introduction of Buddhism had a great impact on the Japanese people, but the Shinto rituals and beliefs have never been replaced.

Most Japanese practice both religions.

How can the Japanese simultaneously practice Buddhism and Shintoism, with their two very different belief structures?

Most Japanese consider Shintoism to be the religion of the living (encompassing celebration of birth, marriage, fertility, health) and Buddhism to be the religion of death (funerals, afterlife, salvation).

The two are not generally viewed as mutually exclusive.

POP QUIZ

What does "Rastafari" mean?

a. Heavenly weed

b. Homeward bound

c. It was the birth name of Ethiopian Emperor Haile Salassie I.

d. It is the city where Bob Marley was born.

ANSWER: c.

Haile Salassie is the name taken by Ras Tafari Makonnen when he rose to power.

Haile Salassie means "Might of the Trinity."

His ascension on November 2, 1930, was seen as the fulfillment of Garvey's prophecy.

According to Marcus Garvey, Africans are the true Israelites who were dispersed to the far corners of the earth as punishment by God.

In the 1920s, Garvey lived in Jamaica, encouraging pride in being black and leading a "Back to Africa" movement.

In 1927, his prophesy ("Look to Africa, for there a king shall be crowned") was part of what led to his being thought of as John the Baptist, *redux*.

Do Rastafarians think that Haile Salassie was God?

Yes, they see him as the messiah and embodiment of God (Jah, short for Jehovah) and his presence as a sign of the beginning of their return to Africa.

Although the Emperor denied any divinity, he facilitated the return to Africa of more than 2,000 blacks with a donation of 500 acres of his own land in 1955.

When he visited Jamaica in 1966, he told the Rastafarians to liberate the people of Jamaica before they left for Ethiopia.

THE GOLDEN RULE,
AS REFLECTED IN MANY OF THE WORLD'S RELIGIONS

CHRISTIANITY

In all things, do to others what you would have them do to you. This is the law and the prophets.

MATTHEW 7:12

CONFUCIANISM

What you don't want done to yourself, don't do to others.

ANALECTS 12:2

BRAHMANISM

This is the sum of dharma (duty): do nothing to others which would be painful if done to you.

MAHABHARATA 5:1517 (HINDU VEDAS)

BUDDHISM

Do not treat others in ways that you yourself would find hurtful.

UDANAVARGA 5:1

ISLAM

None of you is a believer until he desires for his brother that which he desires for himself.

13TH OF 40 HADITHS OF AN-NAWAWI

JAINISM

A man should wander about treating all creatures as he himself would be treated.

SUTRAKRITANGA 1.11.33

JUDAISM

What is hateful to you, do not to your fellow man. This is the law: all the rest is commentary.

HILLEL; TALMUD, SHABBAT 31A

TAOISM

Regard your neighbor's gain as your own gain and your neighbor's loss as your own loss.

LAO TZU, T'AI SHANG KAN YING P'IEN, 213–218

ZOROASTRIANISM

That nature alone is good which refrains from doing to another whatsoever is not good for itself.

DADISTEN-I-DINIK, 94,5

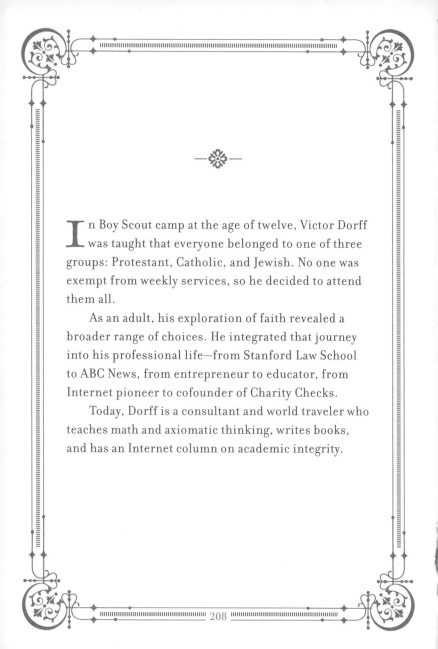

In Boy Scout camp at the age of twelve, Victor Dorff was taught that everyone belonged to one of three groups: Protestant, Catholic, and Jewish. No one was exempt from weekly services, so he decided to attend them all.

As an adult, his exploration of faith revealed a broader range of choices. He integrated that journey into his professional life—from Stanford Law School to ABC News, from entrepreneur to educator, from Internet pioneer to cofounder of Charity Checks.

Today, Dorff is a consultant and world traveler who teaches math and axiomatic thinking, writes books, and has an Internet column on academic integrity.